Benjamin Disraeli

Very Interesting People

*Bite-sized biographies of Britain's most
fascinating historical figures*

Benjamin Disraeli

Very Interesting People

Jonathan Parry

OXFORD
UNIVERSITY PRESS

OXFORD
UNIVERSITY PRESS

Great Clarendon Street, Oxford OX2 6DP

Oxford University Press is a department of the University of Oxford.
It furthers the University's objective of excellence in research, scholarship,
and education by publishing worldwide in

Oxford New York

Auckland Cape Town Dar es Salaam Hong Kong Karachi
Kuala Lumpur Madrid Melbourne Mexico City Nairobi
New Delhi Shanghai Taipei Toronto

With offices in

Argentina Austria Brazil Chile Czech Republic France Greece
Guatemala Hungary Italy Japan Poland Portugal Singapore
South Korea Switzerland Thailand Turkey Ukraine Vietnam

Oxford is a registered trade mark of Oxford University Press
in the UK and in certain other countries

Published in the United States
by Oxford University Press Inc., New York

First published in the *Oxford Dictionary of National Biography* 2004
This paperback edition first published 2007

© Oxford University Press 2007

Database right Oxford University Press (maker)

First published 2007

British Library Cataloguing in Publication Data

Data available

Library of Congress Cataloging in Publication Data

Data available

Typeset by SPI Publisher Services, Pondicherry, India
Printed in Great Britain
on acid-free paper by
Clays Ltd, St Ives plc

ISBN 978–0–19–921359–7 (Pbk.)

10 9 8 7 6 5 4 3 2

Contents

Preface

Benjamin Disraeli remains the most intriguing of nineteenth-century British politicians. He lacked a conventional public school and university background, but by oratory, flair and hard graft he overcame snobbery and anti-semitism to become prime minister for seven years. His epigrams and flamboyance provided a telling contrast not only with his great rival William Gladstone but also with the stolid and insular Conservative MPs that he led. His literary productivity and historical enthusiasms demonstrated his intellectual fertility, yet many contemporaries did not see him as a man of principle, and historians—and subsequent Conservative politicians—have assessed his political philosophy and legacy in profoundly different ways.

This short biography, written originally for the *Oxford Dictionary of National Biography*, offers a guide to his life, ideas and significance. Though primarily chronological, it also explores a number of underlying themes. One is his youthful Romantic desire for fame and belief in his own genius, leading him to abandon a humdrum legal career and launch himself as a novelist. He struggled to reconcile the worlds of imagination and action—his desire for artistic creativity with his strong thirst for political position. His initial attempts to storm the ramparts of British politics were damaged by his self-presentation as an unconventional thinker at least as much as by his lack of connections.

In the 1840s Disraeli developed his ideas in a way more appropriate for an ambitious Conservative MP. This decade of national crisis was the most important influence on his career. He saw the need to attack social divisions by improving the vigour and tone of the governing classes, especially the aristocracy and the Church. He argued that the defence of religion, property and political leadership would benefit from the guidance of insightful minds—like his own—which understood both Jewish philosophy and English history.

As a devoted student of the latter, he also criticized the excessive influence of the commercial classes on current British foreign and colonial policy, which he felt was damaging the national interest and honour. Most of his later political strategies bore some relationship, albeit indirect, to such ideas.

Disraeli once said that his politics could be 'summed up in one word—England'. Patriotism was indeed a feature of many of his initiatives, though often conceived idiosyncratically. As a leader of the Conservative opposition throughout the long period of Liberal political dominance between 1846 and 1874, he tried many political manoeuvres. Marrying low intrigue with high philosophy, they were characteristically fertile and often impractical. Several times he tangled with issues of national religion, which he never understood as well as he thought he did. Finally, as prime minister of a majority Conservative government between 1874 and 1880, he sought to supply national leadership, particularly in foreign policy, in order to restore British greatness and win lasting fame for himself.

Disraeli always looked backwards more than forwards. Arguably he did not understand or seriously court the emerging urban democracy. Yet circumstances have given him a different posthumous image. To suit the interests of the Conservative party after 1881, he was reinvented as a populist, a social reformer and an imperialist. That his career after death has been so long and many-sided is a tribute to the creativity of his mind and the fascination of his life.

Jonathan Parry

August 2006

About the author

Jonathan Parry is a Reader in Modern British History at the University of Cambridge and a Fellow of Pembroke College. His principal publications include *The Rise and Fall of Liberal Government in Victorian Britain* (1993) and *The Politics of Patriotism: English Liberalism, National Identity and Europe, 1830–1886* (2006).

The search for fame

Benjamin Disraeli, earl of
Beaconsfield (1804–1881), prime minister and
novelist, was born on 21 December 1804 at 6
King's Road, Bedford Row, London, the eldest
son and second of five children of Isaac D'Israeli
(1766–1848) and his wife, Maria (1775–1847),
daughter of Naphtali and Ricca Basevi. From 1810
or 1811 he attended a school at Islington kept by
a Miss Roper, and then, probably from 1813, one
at Blackheath belonging to the Revd John Potti-
cary, where he was given separate instruction in
Judaism. However, he was baptized into the Christian faith (as an Anglican) on 31 July 1817 and
thereafter attended a different school, Higham
Hall in Epping Forest, run by the Unitarian minister Eli Cogan, until 1819 or 1820, after which
he was taught at home. The family had moved to

6 Bloomsbury Square after the death of Benjamin's grandfather in 1816 had increased Isaac D'Israeli's means. That death also removed the family's last tie with the Jewish religion and led to the baptism of the children. Isaac was an easy-going Voltairean sceptic whose interests were those of a reclusive literary dilettante and whose friends tended to be London publishers and antiquaries. From an early age Benjamin was introduced to this circle and to his father's extensive and eclectic library, which left a much clearer stamp on his mind and tastes than the more disciplined classical training offered at Higham Hall. Benjamin had dropped the apostrophe in his surname by December 1822, though it was still widely used (for example, in *Hansard*) until the 1840s.

Disraeli in the 1820s

In November 1821 Disraeli was articled at his father's arrangement to a solicitor's firm in the Old Jewry, and spent three years there. Subsequently (in April 1827) his name was entered at Lincoln's Inn, but though he ate dinners for a time, he had rejected the idea of a career at the bar some years before he withdrew his name in November 1831. He had, and retained, a strong dislike of the mundane lifestyle of the English middle classes: for them, 'often the only adventure of life' was marriage (Smith, *Disraeli*, 69). 'To be a great lawyer, I must give up my chance of being a great man' (*Vivian Grey*, bk 1, chap. 9). An ardent admirer of Lord Byron (whom his father knew), he dreamed instead of literary fame. The example of Byron—and of George Canning in politics— showed him how men of unusual charisma and insight could win international admiration with the aid of the burgeoning media. Disraeli fell heavily under the influence of Romanticism. From the early 1820s he had adopted an appropriately eye-catching and narcissistic style of dress, with ruffled shirts, velvet trousers, coloured waistcoats, and jewellery, and he wore his hair in cascades of ringlets. It was on his first continental travels, to Germany in 1824 with his father, that he decided to try to escape from a legal career. The latter parts of his first published novel, *Vivian Grey*, were set in Germany—the home of Goethe, whose *Wilhelm Meister*, translated into English in 1824, clearly influenced his early literary style. A longer tour of the continent in August 1826 included a stay at Geneva, where Disraeli engaged Byron's former boatman to row him on the lake. He reflected self-consciously, in Romantic fashion, on the sublime natural creations that he observed on his travels, and concluded that he loved 'trees better than men' (*Letters*, 1.92).

In May 1824 Disraeli submitted a manuscript to his father's friend John Murray, but it was not published. His attempt over the next year to establish the financial independence necessary for a literary career was a catastrophic failure. With a friend he sought to capitalize on the speculative bubble in South American mining companies. Disraeli also wrote pamphlets puffing the operations. By June 1825 they had lost £7000. A third partner took on much of this debt; Disraeli could not finally settle with him until 1849. Later in 1825 he urged a willing Murray to establish a new morning paper, *The Representative*, to compete with *The Times*. He worked hard on this venture, impressing Murray with his energy and insight, but failed to persuade J. G. Lockhart to take up a major editorial role, and the journal collapsed after six months. Disraeli used this episode in *Vivian Grey*, the first part of which was published anonymously in two volumes in April 1826. It was publicized by the publisher Henry Colburn as a sensational *roman-à-clef* in the then fashionable silver-fork style. It portrayed with intensity the desperate, unscrupulous ambition of a clever young man, and his come-uppance. It also set out a highly irreverent view of London society, exposing the egotism, superficiality, and charlatanism of its members. This combination of unmistakable self-exposure and reckless satire did Disraeli's reputation great and lasting damage—for the identity of the author was soon revealed. The book also earned some damning reviews, which dwelt on its solecisms and general immaturity. Moreover, Murray and Lockhart, men of great influence in literary circles, were deeply offended by the sneering treatment of characters based on them.

The financial disaster and literary abuse to which Disraeli was subjected in 1825–6 almost certainly contributed to the onset of a major nervous crisis that affected him for much of the next four years. He had always been moody, sensitive, and solitary by nature, but now became seriously depressed and lethargic. The 'cold, dull world', he later wrote, could not remotely conceive the 'despondency' of 'youthful genius' that was conscious of 'the strong necessity for fame', yet had 'no simultaneous faith in [its] own power' (*Contarini Fleming*, pt 1, chap. 11).

It was not until a lengthier journey, to the East in 1830–31 (financed partly by a fashionable but light novel, *The Young Duke*, written in 1829–30), that Disraeli finally acquired a strong enough sense of identity to sustain him in his search for fame. Between June and September 1830 he travelled with William Meredith in Gibraltar, Spain, and Malta, where they joined up with James Clay, an Oxford friend of Meredith. Clay's buccaneering temperament, raffish habits, and sexual experience fascinated Disraeli and made the rest of the journey more adventurous. Joined by Byron's former servant Tita Falcieri, the three men toured the Ottoman empire experiencing Eastern lifestyles. Disraeli spent a week at the court of the grand vizier Redschid Ali in Albania, and, after visiting Athens, a further six weeks in Constantinople. The exotic, colourful splendour of Turkish courts appealed immensely to his imagination; he felt that the 'calm and luxurious' existence of the people accorded with his 'indolent and melancholy' tastes (Monypenny and Buckle, 1.159, 170). He loved the duplicitous intrigue of court politics and its distance from the puritanical moralism of the Western bourgeoisie; staying with Redschid, Disraeli wrote of the 'delight of being

made much of by a man who was daily decap-
itating half the province' (ibid., 158). The travellers then proceeded to Jerusalem, where Disraeli
spent a seminal week, before staying five months
in Egypt. The tour was cut short dramatically by
Meredith's death from smallpox in Cairo in July
1831. Disraeli had to be treated for venereal dis-
ease on his return to London.

Like other nineteenth-century travellers to the
East, Disraeli felt enriched by his experiences,
becoming aware of values that seemed denied
to his insular countrymen. The journey encouraged his self-consciousness, his moral relativism,
and his interest in Eastern racial and religious
attitudes. On his return he could strike others as
insufferably affected: according to one account,
he was much given to sticking his fingers in
his lapels and drawling, 'Allah is great' (Bradford, 51). There is a malicious contemporary
portrait of him in dandy mode, as Jericho Jabber
in Rosina Bulwer's *Very Successful* (1856). In
1833 he published a novel, *The Wondrous Tale
of Alroy*, which concerned the dilemma faced
by a twelfth-century Middle Eastern Jew who
sought fame, but who faced conflicting ideals:
between establishing a purely Jewish regime and

a larger empire assimilating other religions. The moral of his failure was that a taste for action and the power of imagination were both needed in a leader. Though neither meritorious nor commercially successful, *Alroy* shows Disraeli thinking about problems that were to concern him a great deal in the future; it portrayed 'my ideal ambition' (Monypenny and Buckle, 1.236).

The other literary product of Disraeli's travels was *Contarini Fleming* (1832). Subtitled 'a psychological autobiography', *Contarini*, like *Vivian Grey*, was a *Bildungsroman* exploring the development of the artistic consciousness and containing much tortured reflection on Disraeli's destiny. It presents the dual nature of the eponymous hero, a man of mixed Mediterranean and northern background, a brooding artist but aspiring man of action, deeply imaginative yet energetic and courageous. Disraeli was very aware of these two sides of his personality. *Contarini* ends on a new theme, the transition of Europe from feudal to federal principles (pt 7, chap. 2). In a diary of 1833 Disraeli claimed that his insights were 'continental' and 'revolutionary' (Monypenny and Buckle, 1.236), by which he presumably meant broad and original enough to encompass the intellectual and social

forces that were shaping Europe. In 1834 he finished a heroic poem, on the scale of Homer and
apparently conceived when standing on the plain
of Troy; its object was to evoke the clash of feudal
and democratic principles in Europe since the
French Revolution. Entitled *The Revolutionary
Epick*, it was not remotely a success, but it testi-
fied to Disraeli's enthusiasm for the fashionable
continental conception that the progress of human
affairs was realized through the interaction of
individual will, ideas, and great social forces.
Disraeli was fascinated by the creativity with
which the greatest statesmen, such as Napoleon,
moulded social change and thus won worldwide
renown.

It was in the early 1830s that Disraeli decided
to begin a political career. In 1833 he recorded
that he would 'write no more about myself'
(Monypenny and Buckle, 1.236); certainly there
seemed little prospect of fame through litera-
ture. His pride sought an existence independent
of the literary pundits and titled and frivolous
patrons who seemed to dictate fortunes in letters. Politics, he later wrote, offered the chance
of 'power o'er the powerful' (*Letters*, 4.250). It
also offered therapeutic excitement: 'action may

not always be happiness, but there is no happiness without action' (*Lothair*, chap. 79). The reform crisis of 1830–32 opened the prospect of political realignments and quick fame for men of resource and vision. The Disraelite hero of *A Year at Hartlebury*, the novel he wrote with his sister and published anonymously in 1834 (and whose authorship was established in 1983 by Ellen Henderson and John P. Matthews), turned, 'at the prospect of insurrection . . . with more affection towards a country he had hitherto condemned as too uneventful for a man of genius' (p. 58). More mundanely, the cost of attempting to cut a dash in society, on top of his incompetent management of his previous debts, ensured that a long queue of creditors hounded him. A seat in parliament offered immunity from imprisonment for debt.

Towards parliament and marriage

Disraeli's first parliamentary candidature was at High Wycombe, the nearest borough to the house at Bradenham that his father rented from 1829. The two sitting MPs were whigs, and one was the son of the local landowner Lord Carrington. It was both necessary and congenial for Disraeli to declare himself an independent radical, opposed to whiggism and oligarchy, at a by-election in June 1832 and then at the general election held on the new franchise in December 1832. On both occasions he was defeated. His friend Edward Lytton Bulwer secured him letters of support from leading radicals Daniel O'Connell and Sir Francis Burdett. As the only opposition candidate, Disraeli naturally courted tory voters, and in 1833, excited by accusations that in doing so he was inconsistent, he published *What is He?*, in which he argued for a tory–radical coalition against the whigs. His background, ostentatious manner, and verbal pyrotechnics ensured that opponents would charge him with lack of principle, but in fact few politicians of the 1830s were more interested than he was in fashioning a coherent individual perspective on politics. Disraeli sought independence from faction and from condescension, and to be noticed; his rise would surely have been more rapid had he made more compromises with the system.

Disraeli's political path began to clear when in 1834 he met one of the few leading tories colourful, indiscreet, and clever enough to appreciate his talents: Lord Lyndhurst. Disraeli was introduced to him by Henrietta Sykes, an older married lady with whom Lyndhurst had been having an increasingly public affair since the summer of 1833. She seems to have cured Disraeli of some immature affectations. It was suspected that he was happy to share Henrietta's affections with Lyndhurst. Certainly the triangular friendship expanded his political circle and lowered her social reputation. Disraeli loved Lyndhurst's gossip and taste for intrigue, and became his secretary and go-between. When he stood again at Wycombe at the 1835 election, once more unsuccessfully, and still as an independent radical, it was with the assistance of £500 from tory funds. The events of this period made it clear that the future lay with a two-party system, and in the spring of 1835 he fought the Taunton by-election as a tory. In March 1836 he was elected to the Carlton Club. Encouraged by Lyndhurst, and invoking the eighteenth-century politician Viscount Bolingbroke as an exemplar, he wrote some vigorous tory propaganda. The most important, his *Vindication of the English Constitution*, was published in December 1835. It used a historical perspective to claim the tories' sympathy with the people, to attack whig, Irish, and utilitarian views, and to assert the legitimacy of the House of Lords' opposition to government policy. More scurrilous were *The Letters of Runnymede*, nineteen anonymous pieces of satire on politicians of the day, which he published in *The Times* in 1836. They included some abuse of the Irish. Disraeli used the whigs' increasingly pro-Catholic Irish policy to justify his toryism, as did the famous former radical Sir Francis Burdett, for whom he canvassed at the Westminster election of 1837. At Taunton in 1835 Disraeli had compared the proposal of Irish church appropriation to the spoliation of the monasteries by the whigs' ancestors. His misreported remarks about O'Connell led the latter to charge him with being a Jew 'of the lowest and most disgusting grade of moral turpitude' (Monypenny and Buckle, 1.288). As on other occasions, Disraeli's pride flared up at such language, and he provoked a public row with O'Connell and his son Morgan, whom he challenged to a duel.

Disraeli was also taken up by Lady Londonderry in the 1836 season, a sign of his increasing reputation in tory circles. He was given a winnable seat at the 1837 election, when he became MP for Maidstone with the other tory candidate, Wyndham Lewis, who lent him money to pay part of the election expenses. Disraeli's debts had grown into a serious problem, and Henrietta's husband's

solicitor had helped him to manage them. However, in late 1836 he terminated the affair with
her; she was very demanding emotionally, and
began a passionate romance with the painter
Daniel Maclise (whose drawing of Disraeli in
1828 effectively recorded his dandyism). Shortly
afterwards Disraeli published *Henrietta Temple*, a
love story and social comedy, and followed it by
Venetia (1837), a portrayal of Byronic existence
in the late eighteenth century, which was written
quickly in order to raise money.

When Wyndham Lewis died suddenly in March
1838, Disraeli consoled his widow, who had been
left with an income of about £5000 per year,
together with their house in London, 1 Grosvenor
Gate. Mary Anne Lewis (1792–1872) was the
daughter of a naval lieutenant and farmer, John
Evans, of Brampford Speke, near Exeter, and
his wife, Eleanor. She was coquettish, impulsive,
not well educated, and extremely talkative, but
also warm, loyal, and sensible. She shared something of Disraeli's love of striking clothes and
social glitter while feeling, like him, an outsider
in very high social circles. Her money, house,
and solid position were undoubtedly attractive
to him (though she had only a life interest

in her husband's estate). But so also were her
vivacity and her childless motherliness. All his
life older women appealed to Disraeli, apparently
in search of a mother-substitute more apprecia-
tive of his genius than his own stolid parent had
been.

Their courtship lasted most of a year, for much
of which time she seems to have been unsure of
his motives. In the end he convinced her of his
genuine emotional attachment; he certainly pur-
sued her ardently. As before when he was absorbed
in passion, he wrote a poetic work, the blank
verse play *The Tragedy of Count Alarcos*, which
was only performed as a curiosity after Disraeli
became prime minister. They were married at
St George's, Hanover Square, on 28 August 1839
and their union thereafter presented a picture of
remarkable mutual devotion and respect. Mary provided the domestic stability and constant admiration that he sorely needed. She also paid off many
of his debts: she had spent £13,000 on these and
his elections by 1842 alone. Like his father's, her
payments would have been more effective had
Disraeli straightened out his affairs, approached
his debts rationally, and been straightforward with
her about the sums owing; instead, his tendency

was to renew his obligations at ruinous interest rates. At the 1841 election his opponent printed posters listing judgments in the courts against Disraeli to the extent of over £22,000, and alleged that he owed at least £6800 more than that.

'Nothing is difficult to the brave'

Backbench rebel, 1837–1846

Disraeli made his maiden speech in parliament on 7 December 1837, in a debate on MPs' privileges. It was another challenge to Daniel O'Connell, the previous speaker, and was hooted down by jeering O'Connellite Irishmen, though not before its extraordinarily elaborate and affected language had caused much hilarity. After that unpropitious beginning Disraeli avoided publicity for most of the rest of the parliament, generally supporting Sir Robert Peel and attacking the free trade agitators. However, he did urge respect for the Chartist movement. Feeling unable to satisfy the financial expectations of the electors of Maidstone, he sought a cheaper seat for the 1841 election; his friend Lord Forester secured him the nomination at Shrewsbury. At this election his crest made its first appearance, with the motto *forti nihil difficile* ('nothing is difficult to the brave').

When Peel became prime minister after the 1841 election, Disraeli sought office from him; unsurprisingly, he did not get it. He continued his support for Peel in 1842 and 1843, seeking fame by attacking the foreign policy of the late government. He blamed the economic depression partly on the whigs' warmongering extravagance and failure to sign a commercial treaty with France. He projected himself as an authority on the needs of British international trade, urging a reversion to the historical policy of commercial diplomacy and reciprocity. He went to France in late 1842 in order to make connections at the court there which would assist his claim to be promoting a new entente with that country. His contacts there—supplied through Bulwer, Count d'Orsay, and Lyndhurst—gained him an audience with Louis Philippe.

In a memorandum to the French king, Disraeli talked of organizing a party of youthful, energetic tory back-benchers in pursuit of a policy sympathetic to France. Though nothing came of this notion as such, it showed his susceptibility to the excitement of high intrigue with a group of youthful men of independence and vision. A small group of such men was in fact forming on the tory benches, inspired by George Smythe, Lord John Manners, and Alexander Baillie-Cochrane. This trio had been at Eton and Cambridge together and had a romantic attachment to the ideals of chivalry, paternalism, and religious orthodoxy which had become fashionable in some landed and university circles in reaction to reform, utilitarianism, and political economy. Disraeli did not adopt all of the specific enthusiasms of Young England, as the group came to be known in 1843. But by the end of the session he was accepted as a fertile contributor to its activities in the House of Commons, and some of the group's enthusiasms rubbed off on him, especially a respect for historic religious ideals evident in his novel, *Sybil*. Over the winter of 1843–4 Disraeli wrote *Coningsby*, his most effective and successful novel to date, a vibrant commentary on the political and social worlds of the 1830s. Featuring the three friends, it gave considerable publicity to the idea of Young England, contrasting its ideals with Peel's lack of principle. Published in May 1844, it quickly sold 3000 copies, for which Disraeli received about £1000.

In 1843 Disraeli offended the Conservative leadership by his vote against the Canada Corn Bill and his speech against Irish coercion. Early in 1844 Peel rebuked him by omitting him from the list of MPs to be summoned to the official party meeting at the start of the session. Over the coming months Disraeli made three speeches containing pointed and sarcastic criticism of the party leadership, such as his attack on its inability to tolerate dissent over the sugar issue.

In October 1844 Disraeli, Manners, and Smythe made successful addresses to young artisans at the Manchester Athenaeum, testifying to the impact made by Young England. While in the north, Disraeli also collected observations about industrial life which he used in *Sybil*, the novel which he wrote over the winter of 1844–5 and published in May 1845, again to considerable interest; it too sold 3000 copies. But Young England broke up in 1845, partly owing to a difference of opinion on the government's proposals for the Maynooth seminary, and partly because of parental pressure on Smythe and Manners not to be disloyal to the party. Meanwhile, Disraeli's abuse of Peel was mounting. In late February he made a celebrated, extended, and neatly vindictive assault on Peel's shiftiness, described by one onlooker as 'aimed with deadly precision', yet delivered with Disraeli's normal 'extreme coolness and impassibility' (Monypenny and Buckle, 2.316). On 17 March he declared that a 'Conservative government is an organised hypocrisy' (*Selected Speeches*, 1.80). His opposition to the Maynooth grant (11 April) was similarly based on the argument that Peel cared nothing for tory principles and sought to extend the 'police surveillance' of Downing Street to entrap Irish Catholics, when they required independence and respect (ibid., 88). By the end of the 1845 session Disraeli had become a celebrated orator. He undoubtedly helped to stimulate the questioning of Peel's trustworthiness on the back benches. Yet he stood essentially alone, without allies, and in such circumstances his capacity to tolerate abuse and short-term political injury is testimony to his remarkable self-confidence and self-reliance.

Disraeli's position was transformed by the events of late 1845, which brought Peel to the Commons in January 1846 as an advocate of repealing the corn laws, in defence of which the vast majority of tory MPs had been elected in 1841. Disraeli seized the initiative against him with a stinging attack

(22 January), accusing him of betraying 'the independence of party' and thus 'the integrity of public men, and the power and influence of Parliament itself' (*Selected Speeches*, 1.110). Now, suddenly, he was no longer alone, as Lord George Bentinck and Lord Stanley took the lead in organizing party opposition to the repeal, while in the constituencies there was an active protectionist campaign. In his speeches on the subject in 1846 Disraeli reiterated his earlier arguments in favour of the historic policy of multilateral tariff reductions through treaty diplomacy. But his greatest contribution to the movement against Peel continued to be his scathing attacks on the latter's inability to uphold the principles of the territorial constitution on which toryism must rest. This was expressed most devastatingly in his famous denunciation of Peel's career as a 'great Appropriation Clause' in his speech on the second reading of the repeal bill on 15 May, which roused the back benches to extraordinary fervour (ibid., 170). Later in the month he lied to the Commons in denying Peel's charge that he had sought office from him in 1841, but Peel was unable or unwilling to capitalize on this, a mark of his powerlessness to deal with Disraeli's invective. As the session continued, Disraeli had hopes of a coalition between protectionist tories

and some whigs and Irish MPs in defence of a compromise tariff. But corn law repeal passed the Lords in late June. On the same night the leading protectionists, including Disraeli, voted with the opposition to defeat Peel's Irish Coercion Bill, on the grounds that the lack of necessity for it had been demonstrated by the long delay in promoting it. Peel resigned, and Disraeli's fame—for good and ill—was assured.

Tory prophet: race and Jewishness

In the 1840s Disraeli wrote three major novels (*Coningsby*, *Sybil*, and *Tancred*, 1847), worked on his biography of Lord George Bentinck (1852), and delivered many ambitious speeches. This output, together with his earlier political comment, helps to chart the progress of his ideas.

Disraeli had begun political life as a proud Romantic individualist with radical leanings, standing 'for myself' rather than any party (Ridley, 112). This was a sign of his youthful arrogance, but also a typical declaration against what radicals saw as whig factionalism and falseness. Gifted with an ability to expose the selfish and hypocritical underbelly of the glittering social and political world, he shared the views of those who saw the whigs as frauds who had arrogated the title of the popular party when they were in fact a 'Venetian' oligarchy. After he had adopted tory colours, Disraeli continued—especially in *Sybil*—to portray the whigs as a rapacious clique of great families, who had secured their hold on power by their canting claim to be protecting the civil and religious liberties of the people from attack in 1688–9. He asserted that popular liberties in fact rested on the territorial constitution—on the land, the church, and other interests whose vitality prevented central government despotism. The Venetian instincts of eighteenth-century whigs had crippled the country with heavy indirect taxes levied in order to fight unnecessary wars and to siphon off rewards for themselves. The one man who might have moralized whig misrule—the outsider–prophet Edmund Burke—was refused a cabinet place by these snobs, and in his vengeance turned his eloquence against them, thereby helping to keep them out of power for forty-five years. It was only the blunders of William Pitt's heirs that gave the whigs the opportunity to mount an audacious *coup d'état* in 1830 and once again to restrict power to an aristocratic clique by claiming to follow libertarian sentiments. Their true intentions were seen in their centralizing initiatives of the 1830s with regard to the poor law, education, and policing, all of which Disraeli criticized. They also had to be opposed for their exclusiveness, their incapacity, and their willingness to consort with destructive allies, particularly O'Connell.

Here and on other subjects Disraeli derived his arguments from books—mainly from Burke and tory historians, and Thomas Carlyle and Germanic writers—and from the literary and religious interests of his father. But he assembled and developed his ideas in an inimitable confection, and with a degree of purpose rare among parliamentarians. He thought of himself as a prophet of deep insights who had arrived at his opinions by 'reading and thought' rather than having 'had hereditary opinions carved out' for him (Monypenny and Buckle, 2.371). As he commented with respect to Christ, all the great minds were formed in seclusion (*Disraeli's Reminiscences*, ed. H. M. Swartz and M. Swartz, 1975, 8).

For Disraeli historical and sociological awareness was necessary in order to govern men. In particular, 'all is race' (Disraeli, *Bentinck*, 331);

the values of each race determined its past and prospects. Some races were superior; others were degraded (by interbreeding or luxury) and would be conquered. Conquest was a natural objective of races such as the Slavs. But Disraeli was most concerned with two other races: the Semites (especially the Jews) and the English. These were races that understood the essence of civilization: the Jewish values of 'religion, property, and natural aristocracy' (ibid., 497). 'A civilised community must rest on a large realised capital of thought and sentiment; there must be a reserved fund of public morality to draw upon....Society has a soul as well as a body' (Disraeli, *Inaugural Address*, 15). The alternative to government in tune with indigenous traditions was a resort to a 'philosophic' or 'cosmopolitan' basis—to abstract theories, such as 'cosmopolitan fraternity' and the equality of man, 'pernicious' doctrines that would 'deteriorate the great races and destroy all the genius of the world' (Disraeli, *Bentinck*, 496). Republicanism and socialism involved a relapse into 'primitive...savagery' (ibid., 509), though their vitality and appeal were all too comprehensible. One reason for their attraction was that men, who were 'made to adore and obey', had been failed by their political and religious leaders and left to 'find a chieftain in [their] own passions' (*Coningsby*, bk 4, chap. 13). A nation that had 'lost its faith in religion is in a state of decadence' (*Selection from the Diaries of…Derby*, 97). Modern Europe had fallen victim to materialism: it had mistaken comfort for civilization (*Tancred*, bk 3, chap. 7). Disraeli drew two conclusions. A properly run society was necessarily élitist: 'the Spirit of the Age is the very thing that a great man changes' (*Coningsby*, bk 3, chap. 1). And it must rest on the national, not the cosmopolitan, principle.

It followed that England should venerate the Jews, who understood all this. They represented the 'Semitic principle—all that is spiritual in our nature' (Disraeli, *Bentinck*, 496), being descended from the Arabian peoples to whom divine truth had been revealed and who had founded the great religions. The Christian church in particular was completed Judaism, a 'sacred corporation for the promulgation and maintenance in Europe of certain Asian principles…of divine origin and of universal and eternal application' (*Coningsby*, preface to 5th edn, 1849). Jesus and the Virgin Mary were Jews. 'Half Christendom worships a Jewess and the other half a Jew.…Which do you think should be the superior race; the worshipped or the worshippers?' (*Tancred*, bk 3, chap. 4). The Roman church had been founded by a Hebrew when the English were 'tattooed savages' (ibid., bk 2, chap. 11), and the crusades, by bringing medieval Westerners to Jerusalem, had renewed Asia's spiritual hold on Europe. The Arabs, 'Jews on horseback', retained much of the spiritual sense, social cohesion, and harmony with nature that the West so badly needed to rediscover. The hero of *Tancred* goes to Jerusalem in an attempt to penetrate and draw spiritual sustenance from 'the great Asian mystery' (bk 2, chap. 11; bk 4, chap. 3). Disraeli convinced himself (wrongly) that he derived from the Sephardi aristocracy of Iberian Jews driven from Spain at the end of the fifteenth century. The English aristocracy, he pointed out, were descended merely from 'a horde of Baltic pirates' (Blake, 203).

Presenting himself as Jewish symbolized Disraeli's uniqueness when he was fighting for respect, and explained his set-backs. Presenting Jewishness as aristocratic and religious legitimized his claim to understand the perils facing modern England and to offer 'national' solutions to them. English toryism was 'copied from the mighty [Jewish] prototype' (*Coningsby*, bk 4, chap. 15). Disraeli was thus able to square his Jewishness with his equally deep attachment to England and her history. Hardly any nineteenth-century politician was more deeply enthused by the English past; he almost never made a significant speech without invoking it, and talked at length about local history to visitors to his house at Hughenden. Remodelling the house in 1862–3 'realised a romance' to restore its pre-civil war appearance, including a garden of terraces 'in which cavaliers might roam' (Monypenny and Buckle, 3.472). On leaving office in 1852 he disobeyed the custom of passing on the chancellor of the exchequer's gown to his successor (William Gladstone); instead, he kept it until the end of his life because it had been worn by his hero Pitt.

England in crisis

Disraeli believed that England's history explained her greatness, and that her future greatness depended on the maintenance of her constitutional traditions. In the aftermath of the 1848 revolutions England was the 'only important European community that is still governed by traditionary influences' (Disraeli, *Bentinck*, 555).

These influences were 'bulwarks of the multitude' against the destructive despotism of an over-mighty central government (*Lothair*, general preface to 1870 edn); they included the Church of England, the ancient universities, the principles of historic parties, and the 'noble system of self-government' (*Selected Speeches*, 2.455). Local self-government and parliamentary government were essential aspects of England's strength; her uniqueness was that 'society has always been more powerful than the State', thus guaranteeing order and liberty (*The Times*, 18 June 1868, 9).

At times in the 1840s Disraeli argued that these constitutional and social traditions were collapsing, and with them the character of England as a community. In *Tancred* he wrote that 'the people of this country have ceased to be a nation' (bk 2, chap. 1). Parliament no longer represented a 'disciplined array of traditionary influences' but a bundle of crotchets and ambitions, incapable of reaching agreement on an organic, spiritual, or elevating artistic policy (*Selected Speeches*, 2.455). *Tancred* in particular is very critical of the decay of the historic parliamentary ideal, reflecting the shortcomings, successively, of Peel's autocracy and Lord John Russell's minority government. (At this juncture Disraeli even played with the possibility that the monarchy, buttressed by a free press, might represent the national will better, a view raked up and used against him by his opponents at the 1880 election.) But the fundamental problem was social disorganization, with materialism and religious sectarianism following in its wake. The church is portrayed, in *Sybil* and *Tancred*, as riddled with small-minded compromisers incapable of touching the heart of nations. *Sybil* dwells on the immoral brutality of working-class life in manufacturing and inner-city areas untouched by upper-class guidance; this was the abnegation of civilization. He attacked the exploitation of labour, whether by selfish industrialists or by squires imbued with the doctrine of political economy; both reduced human relations to the cash nexus. Yet Disraeli was equally critical of the sybaritic and insular English aristocracy, ignorant, pampered, obsessed with trivialities, and instinctively exclusive and oppressive in their political responses. A return to the old feudalism was not possible. Manchester, he wrote in *Coningsby*, was the Athens of the scientific age (bk 4, chap. 1). It represented ideas which would not go away; politicians had to deal with them.

The 1840s presented a further danger, an international one. Disraeli appropriated Burkean anti-Jacobin polemic in arguing that the difference between tory and whig/Liberal government was the difference between government on the national and on the cosmopolitan principle—a view that he reiterated throughout his career. This analysis relied mainly on the fact that the whigs were allied to O'Connellite Catholics, dissenters, Cobdenite internationalists, and, later, a handful of republicans and atheists. In the 1840s the main 'cosmopolitan' threat presented by the Liberal forces in parliament came from the Cobdenite free-traders who naïvely claimed that their principles would promote 'peace and plenty' when the world was 'in arms' (Monypenny and Buckle, 3.97). Disraeli was profoundly alarmed by the insularity of commercial opinion in England, because it would prevent an intelligent European policy counteracting corrosive democratic principles. In 1848–9 he repeated the view of the *Revolutionary Epick*, that Europe was declining from feudal into federal, republican American-style politics (ibid., 166, 178). But he thought that the transatlantic model would not work there because of the debris left behind by traditionary influences, and that the resulting disturbances would have to be suppressed by military power, by vast standing armies (Disraeli, *Bentinck*, 554–5). Europe faced a future alternating between revolution and Russian-influenced militarism, unless Britain co-operated with France and/or Austria to defend traditional values. (He admired the former Austrian chancellor, Metternich, with whom he had several conversations after 1848.) 'Once destroy the English aristocracy, and enthrone the commercial principle as omnipotent in this island', and nothing can stop 'the Slavonians conquering the whole of the South of Europe' (Monypenny and Buckle, 3.195). Paradoxically but crucially, Disraeli interpreted British isolationism as cosmopolitanism, and believed that a vigorous continental policy was necessary to prevent the triumph in Britain and Europe of cosmopolitan principles.

There is no reason to doubt Disraeli's pessimism about the state of England in this crisis-ridden decade; many shared it. However, the crisis was also convenient, because it pointed up the need for leadership capable of making England a nation again. Ideally, such a man would have the insight and imagination of Sidonia, the Jewish sphinx of the novels, who could solve 'with a phrase some deep problem that men muse over for years' (*Coningsby*, bk 3, chap. 1). He need not be personally religious, as long as he understood the importance of religion to the English. Many passages in *Sybil* admire the medieval spirit—of mutual obligation within a powerful religious framework. But these passages sought to make a point about the English character rather than to prescribe a particular religious solution. Disraeli himself, though interested in theological subjects and a practising Anglican, told the fifteenth earl of Derby in 1872 that he was 'personally incapable of religious belief' (*Selection from the Diaries of…Derby*, 97). In *Tancred* he defined faith as 'inward and personal energy in man' (bk 2, chap. 14). But though the novels were in one sense a personal manifesto of an ambitious man, this view gains from retrospect. Disraeli, a very marginal figure when he wrote *Coningsby* and *Sybil*, believed that the natural leaders of society were 'the gentlemen of England' (Monypenny and Buckle, 3.101). The novels urged young men of property, energy, and vision to enter politics to defend their heritage. Disraeli always idealized such men, and *Sybil* ends with a rallying cry to the nation's youth, 'the trustees of Posterity'.

Disraeli's principles were general and intended to apply in a variety of circumstances; that is why they may appear insubstantial. He never diverged from his broad assumptions about tradition, leadership, cosmopolitanism, and national dissolution, or from his belief that politics involved applying the first two concepts to defeat the second two. But the form in which challenges to national harmony and greatness arose necessarily changed over time; and for Disraeli the art of politics was the settlement of specific problems as they emerged. In the 1840s the overwhelming difficulty was the unrest of the Chartists and the Anti-Corn Law League. In the 1860s and 1870s the greatest threat was to religion at home and abroad, from atheism and church factionalism. In the 1870s and 1880s the major danger was the international challenge to property. In foreign affairs there was a constant problem about British commercial isolationism and an intermittent one about the destabilizing effect on Europe of Palmerstonian Liberal interventionism. For most of his life, also, Disraeli was out of power, and confined to the luxury of criticizing the inadequate leadership skills of others. *Coningsby* contains no definite solutions to the crisis of the 1840s, merely a demand for firm, responsive government to reduce social tension. None the less, in his attack on Peel can be discerned Disraeli's general conception of toryism—which, he wrote in the *Vindication*, should embody 'the national will and character' (p. 193).

To Disraeli historic toryism involved a defence of the territorial constitution and local independence against centralization; a hostility to Venetian borough-mongering (and therefore a Pittite willingness to contemplate parliamentary reform); a reliance on direct as well as indirect taxation; the pursuit of international commercial advantage by traditional tariff diplomacy; a peaceful but shrewd foreign policy; and the firm but inclusive government of Ireland, rescuing its Catholics from the Cromwellian/whig puritanical yoke. But the mistake of the long conflict with France had overtaxed the country and forced farmers into expensive mortgages; Lord Liverpool, the 'Arch-Mediocrity', had rejected Pitt's youthful sympathy with the people and his support for Catholic emancipation, and had fallen back on repression; the duke of Wellington had fashioned an absurdly exclusive and arrogant image of government which had alienated the aristocracy and middle classes and had allowed the whigs to mount their *coup d'état* in 1830. His successor Peel had failed to demonstrate an understanding of history, a loyalty to party tradition, or any power of imagination. Lacking historical insight or intellectual independence, he had swallowed fashionable cosmopolitan ideas, which he disguised with displays of urbane plausibility and empty rhetoric. In assuming that men could be governed by adjusting tables of import duties and other expedients, he was a symbol of the artificiality and rootlessness of politics in a materialistic age. And, lacking real leadership skills, he had resorted to the 'intolerable yoke of official despotism' to retain power (*Selected Speeches*, 1.97). This attempt to check dissent betrayed back-benchers' honour and party principle, the 'realised experience of our ancient society' (ibid., 2.455). The job of the tory party was to uphold the aristocratic settlement of the country in the impending struggle with the democratic principle (Monypenny and Buckle, 3.125, 134).

Disraeli was equally definite in defending the idea of protection. But for him it was a great historic concept, a crucial aspect of constitutional, imperial, and foreign policy. He had consistently argued in favour of a policy of regulating tariffs by treaties of reciprocity; these also reduced foreign tension and allowed lower defence expenditure. As for the empire, relations with the white settler colonies were in flux in the 1840s as the idea of responsible government developed. Disraeli wanted them to be regularized on a coherent basis, with an imperial tariff, a code for colonial defence, and representatives attending a council in the metropolis. He spoke repeatedly in later years of his sadness that this had not happened. In December 1851 he proposed that in any scheme of parliamentary reform at Westminster the colonial chambers should elect their own representatives, on the lines of the United States senate; this might revive their affection for Britain. The failure to bring about that outcome led Disraeli to lament the collapse of real power over the self-governing colonies—especially when he was chancellor of the exchequer, dealing with the consequences of the whigs' failure to get them to accept the burden of their own defence. He even remarked, impatiently, 'what is the use of these colonial deadweights which *we do not govern*?' (Monypenny and Buckle, 4.476). (This remark has been misinterpreted by many critical commentators to indicate a general lack of commitment to empire.) It was crucial that India and Ireland did not go the same way; Britain must exercise firm but inclusive government over them. In 1844 Disraeli urged that Ireland needed a stronger, more comprehensive executive, just administration, and equality of treatment for all religions. In both places an amicable treatment of the diverse religious groups was the only way to prevent them from developing grievances that might lead them to coalesce against the governing power.

Disraeli was obviously motivated by personal ambition in moving to the tories and in attacking Peel over the corn laws and Irish policy. Equally, he was no unprincipled charlatan. For him the fascination of politics was the simultaneous opportunity that it offered for intrigue as well as the formulation of high policy. The basis of his admiration for Edmund Burke was his ability to combine the two goals, to inspire men with ideals while manoeuvring for the advantage of his party connection. Disraeli's élitist conception of politics attached great importance to the role of individuals in making initiatives, patiently constructing alliances, holding parties together, and dividing opponents. The tension between intrigue and idealism is a major theme in *Tancred*, which is in part a dialogue between Tancred, an imaginative young English aristocrat, and Fakredeen, an emir of Lebanon. Tancred is an ingenuous idealist disgusted with the sordidness of British parliamentary life. Fakredeen has a deep understanding of human nature, honed by years of manoeuvre to evade his creditors. He is vain, reckless, and desperate for all Europe to talk of him. He uses his imaginative understanding in reckless intrigue. Tancred says that only faith, not intrigue, will conquer the imagination of public opinion; but he is too ingenuous for the modern world. Fakredeen argues that 'England won India by intrigue ... intrigue has gained half the thrones of Europe' (bk 3, chap. 5); but he can also see the attraction of principles. The ideal statesman would combine both.

The resolution of the crisis of 1845–6 left Disraeli a leading figure in the Conservative Party, whose role as the defender of aristocratic ideals in British politics he henceforth upheld vigorously. Unfortunately, the protectionists were in a minority, needing to make alliances in order to exercise power, with the danger that those coalitions might swamp them or cause them to betray their principles. In September 1846 Disraeli wrote that an alliance between the protectionists and the 'real whigs' in defence of the territorial constitution and strong, inclusive government was the natural solution to the problems of Britain and Ireland (*Letters*, 4.258). He was equally aware of the enormous obstacles to this solution, among them the instinctive protectionism and 'No Popery' of the tory back benches. Could Conservatives—could he—manoeuvre towards power without damaging the party's independence and ideals? The rest of this book charts Disraeli's attempt to reconcile intrigue with imagination and ideas in that objective. It would be an absorbing task for a man of action. After 1846 Disraeli would not need to retreat into fictional worlds in order to find something to manipulate.

A restless tactician

3

Political leadership, 1847–1852

The Conservative Party split elevated Disraeli to
the front opposition bench in 1847. This completed a change of parliamentary image: colourful
attire had by now given way to the black frock
coat (sometimes blue in summer), grey trousers,
plush waistcoat, and sober neckerchief which was
to be his Commons uniform for the next thirty
years. He worked hard on his oratory, mugging
up blue books and spending all day memorizing
figures so that his mastery of them in debate
could seem as spontaneous as Peel's. He capitalized
on his clear voice, great command of language,
and extraordinarily retentive memory, and now
began to learn the art of managing parliamentary
debates tactically. Lord George Bentinck, the protectionists' leader in the Commons, regarded him

as an indispensable lieutenant. And his new eminence in a landed party allowed him to abandon the vexations of a borough seat to become MP for Buckinghamshire at the 1847 election; he retained the seat, usually unopposed, until he became a peer in 1876. He had been a justice of the peace in Buckinghamshire since 1836 and a deputy lieutenant since 1845.

Most significantly for his lifestyle, Disraeli acquired the small country house of Hughenden Manor, outside High Wycombe, in late 1848. The purchase was negotiated by Philip Rose, a lawyer and Buckinghamshire neighbour, whom Disraeli had placed in charge of his financial affairs in 1846. Hughenden was not a large house, and the estate ran only to 750 acres (later increased to 1400 by enclosures and purchases). None the less, it was way beyond his means when he agreed to buy it for £35,000 in March 1847; his wife's income was already heavily burdened by his debt repayments. The money was to come from his father and from Bentinck and his two brothers, who were anxious to establish Disraeli as a landowner MP. The purchase was delayed for over a year while the financial details were sorted out; in the event Disraeli's father and Bentinck both died before it was

completed. Despite a small legacy from Isaac, the
transaction ended with Disraeli owing Bentinck's
brothers £25,000. In 1857 the outstanding money
was called in by the elder brother, now duke of
Portland, who disliked Disraeli's politics; he had
to resort once more to moneylenders.

Hughenden was an essential status symbol for
Disraeli, but he also gained spiritual succour in
this adopted homeland. His was not a typical
arrivisme; it was an affair of the inward imagination rather than one of outward snobbery. Though
he liked to wear the clothes of a country sportsman
(initially with excessive zeal), he neither shot nor
hunted and disliked country-house visiting with
its conventions, its 'constant dressing & indiges-
tion' (*Letters*, 5.210), and its masculine conversations. Mary Anne and he did not entertain very
much at Hughenden, at least in the early years
(though their Buckinghamshire neighbours the
Rothschilds were frequent visitors). The house's
attraction was that it gave him roots in England, allowing him to place himself in a tradition of defenders of property and civilization, and
thus focusing his Burkean sentiments. Hence his
love of his woods, a symbol of permanence; he
prided himself on the number of trees he planted,

persuaded visitors to add specimens, and carried a small hatchet on his estate inspections with which to strip ivy from the bark. His homely estate— with its terrace of peacocks and its little pond presided over by the swans Hero and Leander— and his spacious library (greatly enhanced by his father's death in January 1848) were appropriate settings for self-conscious reflection on the long continuum of English history and his own place in it. For all that, Disraeli frequently found the isolation of Hughenden stifling, especially at times of marital tension or political frustration. He needed the bustle and excitement of London public life in order to raise his spirits.

Fervent protectionism and protestantism made the party difficult to lead. An early test of protestant feeling came with a Commons motion in December 1847 for the removal of Jewish civil and political disabilities. Disraeli took this opportunity to articulate his defence of the Jews as proto-Christians. This argument, met by silence and private anger on the protectionist benches, did his prospects little good. However, Bentinck's support for the same motion led to a rebellion against his leadership and his resignation in December 1847, which created a vacuum. Since it was impossible to find an alternative with the fervour and talent of Bentinck and Disraeli, the two men remained informally in charge of strategy throughout the 1848 session. When Bentinck died suddenly in September 1848, Disraeli was bereft of his strongest supporter; he showed the debt he owed to Bentinck by writing an eloquent and reverential biography, published in December 1851 (1852 on the title page). Yet Bentinck's death also left Disraeli unchallenged as the party's most vigorous debater. However, his status, reputation, and opinions prevented the protectionists from formally nominating him to replace Bentinck. Moreover, Lord Stanley in the Lords, the unquestioned leader of the whole party because of his great social position, ability, and experience, knew that Disraeli's behaviour to Peel had made him unacceptable to the Peelites, whose allegiance Stanley was trying to win. On the other hand, Disraeli refused to serve under any other protectionist, even had any been suitable. The upshot, in January 1849, was the proposal by Stanley of a committee of three: Disraeli, the marquess of Granby, and John Charles Herries. Disraeli was too proud to declare his acceptance of this situation, but Stanley pointed out that he would in practice be leader, and this was generally recognized well before the end of the 1849 session; the committee maintained a shadowy existence until Granby resigned from it at the beginning of 1852.

Chancellor of the exchequer: abandoning protection

Disraeli recognized that a return to the corn laws was politically impossible, since too many mainstream politicians feared the radical social and political reaction that would follow their revival. Upholding protection would confirm the Conservatives' minority status in the country and scare off potential parliamentary allies. He sought a difficult balancing act, trying to find a broader fiscal strategy that would compensate the economic, social, and colonial interests that protection had benefited, yet which would also settle the fiscal question on a 'national' basis, terminating 'the unhappy quarrel between town and country' (*Selected Speeches*, 1.323). He was also worried that, in the agricultural depression of the late 1840s, farmers were being wooed away from the landed interest by the appeals of financial reformers. Restlessly and experimentally, he proposed various fiscal remedies, principally rate relief for agriculture, but also malt tax reduction and income tax differentiation in favour of tenant farmers. Disraeli unsuccessfully opposed the repeal of the navigation laws in 1849—with the result that a grateful shipowner named a 400 ton vessel after him in the following year. He also angrily attacked the 'thoughtless societies out of doors' which were agitating for the return of protection (ibid., 322).

But Stanley rebuked him and declared uncompromisingly for protection, deeming it to be essential for the honour of himself and his party. In the short term Stanley's strategy was the only feasible one, on tactical and principled grounds, and Disraeli was forced to be more equivocal in his public statements. When the Liberal government was defeated in February 1851, no public man outside protectionist ranks would join Stanley, who felt that he must reject the queen's request to form a government—to Disraeli's great annoyance. The following February the Liberals fell more conclusively, and Stanley, now fourteenth earl of Derby, formed a government on the basis that protectionist legislation would not be attempted unless a majority was secured at an election to be held in the summer. At that election (at which Disraeli made only the vaguest reference to protection) no majority was forthcoming, and protection was finally laid to rest in a debate in November 1852, marked by taunts and a crude antisemitic jibe levelled at Disraeli by the Peelite Sidney Herbert.

Disraeli was leader of the House of Commons and chancellor of the exchequer in the 1852 government. Derby had little choice but to give him high office, though his view of him remained equivocal. He appreciated Disraeli's hard work and oratorical ability, but lamented his restlessness as a tactician, and did not invite him to his residence, Knowsley Hall in Lancashire, until late 1853—and then for a dressing-down. Disraeli waived his claim to the leadership in the hope of securing Palmerston's allegiance, but the latter refused to join the cabinet. Disraeli also professed unease that his first government post should be at the Treasury despite his financial ignorance, but Derby told him: 'You know as much as Mr. Canning did. They give you the figures' (Monypenny and Buckle, 3.344). He introduced a provisional budget in April 1852 which extended the income tax for a year; he hoped that a consensus would meanwhile emerge in favour of a more permanent settlement. There was little enthusiasm on the government benches for his speech, which made few concessions to protectionist ideas.

Disraeli's major test came in December, when he was forced (by Peelite pressure) to introduce another budget in the light of the abandonment of protection. This placed him in an almost impossible position. He had to enthuse his back-benchers while not alienating the Liberal majority in the Commons. He made his task harder by opting for an ambitious budget which might give the government momentum for the session. Politically, he could not afford to give landowners rate relief, since this would open him to the charge of class favouritism. But this abandonment of proposals made in opposition, which he justified by pointing to the 20 per cent fall in the cost of poor relief since 1848, was unpopular with his back-benchers. Instead, he offered them a halving of the malt tax, which would also please the urban beer drinker, and coupled this with a staged reduction of the tea duty. In order to pay for this and what he hoped would be a popular reduction of the income tax, he extended the house tax (which had been reintroduced the previous year). This move, unattractive to urban voters, might have been mitigated by a reduction in income tax, but the war scare resulting from Louis Napoleon's imperial pretensions forced the government to increase defence estimates in the autumn and so prevented this. He fell back on the expedient of differentiating between categories of income, proposing to tax farmers and salary-earners at a lower rate, while at the same time bringing more people into the tax net and extending it to Ireland. This complex scheme offended too many interest groups. Opposition MPs had no difficulty in finding enough criticisms of it to justify combining in a negative vote. The government was defeated and resigned.

Disraeli's ten-month spell in office was very important in his career. His ability had been widely recognized and he had become a national figure: he even earned a place at Madame Tussaud's shortly afterwards. (Gladstone did not appear until 1870.) In 1853 he took advantage of this fame to bring out a shilling edition of his novels (including a drastically revised *Vivian Grey*); this sold 300,000 copies in a year. His leading position in the Conservative Party was more secure, now that protection had been abandoned and the Peelites had offended many Conservatives by their behaviour. Nominated by Derby, the university's new chancellor, he was made a doctor of civil law at Oxford University in 1853, and his appearance was much cheered by tory undergraduates. However, this eminence had been achieved at a considerable cost to his reputation. Die-hard protectionists blamed the chancellor of the exchequer above all for the abandonment of their creed, while the Jewish issue prevented him from pleasing ultra-protestants even had he sought to do so. He told Lord Henry Lennox that both these old tory principles were 'exclusive and limited...clearly unfitted for a great and expanding country' (Monypenny and Buckle, 3.383). Yet he was also demonized by the Peelites and their allies in the press as a man of low birth who had goaded the squirearchy against the martyred Peel only to surrender to the wisdom of his policy. In 1854 a member of what Disraeli called 'the Peel school' (in fact, Thomas Macknight) anonymously published a long and venomous *Literary and Political Biography* of him, which capitalized on the awkward incidents in his past (ibid., 3.531). Conservatives who sought reunion regarded him as the symbol of party disunity. Disraeli's reputation never recovered from opponents' interpretations of his political behaviour between 1846 and 1852, though his most visible political trait in these years was, arguably, excitable naïvety rather than fiendish cunning.

The Conservative Party was now to be in opposition for over five years, to Disraeli's frustration. He was furious when, on the fall of the earl of Aberdeen's coalition in early 1855, Derby gave up the queen's commission to form a government once Palmerston had declined to serve under him. Disraeli had concluded that, by taking office at that point, the party might get the credit for a satisfactory conclusion to the Crimean war and force the other conservative influences in politics—principally Palmerston and Gladstone—to accept its dominance. However, Derby thought that public opinion would demand Palmerston as minister, if only until disillusioned, and he was only too aware how opposed the leading Peelites would be to serving with Disraeli.

Throughout these years Disraeli also encountered a lot of distrust from Conservative MPs, despite purging the old protectionist influence in the whips' office and appointing Sir William Jolliffe as chief whip. Derby—hardly a sociable leader himself—criticized his aloofness and unwillingness to court back-benchers. A good part of the unrest was due to Disraeli's insatiable enthusiasm for planning parliamentary sorties against the governments of Aberdeen and Palmerston in the company of other amenable factions, whether Irishmen, radicals, or opposition Liberals. Such tactics were temperamentally irresistible to him, but they were hardly unusual for an opposition leader, and were indeed inevitable in this decade of ideological confusion and ego-ridden intra-party factionalism. Disraeli bewildered his more unimaginatively stolid back-benchers by his sudden parliamentary attacks, which gave further ammunition to his party critics, for whom he remained 'the Jew' (Monypenny and Buckle, 4.44). He appeared to them to be consorting with dangerous radical opinion, at a time of widespread fear in propertied circles of the growing power of 'middle-class' 'Manchester' sentiment, which might undermine the social as well as the political position of the aristocracy.

A Conservative cree not just a tactical
However,   Disr of mystery helped to obscure
opportun

his motives. On the four issues which most preoccupied him, he was working out a more or less coherent Conservative creed. His policies had the great merit to him of appealing beyond the party, but also of upholding a historically coherent position that was viable for a modern empire. Those four issues—finance, foreign policy, India, and parliamentary reform—need to be examined in turn. Though they added to disquiet about him, they also formed the basis of his position over the next fifteen years, especially during the minority government of 1858–9, when he was again chancellor of the exchequer and leader of the Commons.

On finance and foreign policy Disraeli fell foul of the 'John Bull' wing of the party. He saw the political attraction of reducing taxation and appreciated that, if the Conservatives returned to office, a bold and popular budget would be the best way of strengthening their position in the Commons. M~ ~ MPs disliked the income tax, and after 1855 Disrae~ ~ght, more assiduously than Gladstone, to uphold h~ ~er's plans of 1853 for its progressive reduction ~ ~ntual abolition. Disraeli's own budget of Apr~ ~reduced income tax to 5d., while he postpon~ ~duction of the national debt. As a result, in the winter of 1858–9 he was a critic of the renewed war scare and of those Conservatives who advocated a large reconstruction of the navy. Unluckily, his plans for a tax-cutting budget in 1859, repealing the paper duties as well as lowering income tax, were scuppered by Derby's insistence on naval expansion but also, in the event, by the fall of the government before the budget could be presented.

Disraeli's hostility to defence panics was in line with his dislike of emotional popular Francophobia (though he was flexible enough to be able to justify his vote against Palmerston on the Orsini affair in 1858, which brought the Conservatives into government). He made frequent attempts to ingratiate himself and his party with Napoleon III, as he had with Louis Philippe before 1848. To this end he used Ralph Earle, a young and unscrupulous employee of the British embassy at Paris who became Disraeli's private secretary (1858–66), and whom he sent for confidential negotiations of a highly impractical kind. Advocating a cordial relationship with France secured common ground with Peelites and radicals who criticized Palmerston's chauvinism (though Palmerston himself also upheld cordiality when it suited him). But Disraeli also defended the French entente on historical grounds. He adhered to it almost unvaryingly throughout his life, as a way of keeping defence expenditure low while allowing Britain influence in Europe and preventing a damaging general war, which threatened to undermine the balance of power and to unleash revolutionary influences on continental states. Disraeli had innate respect for Palmerston's active involvement in Europe in the teeth of commercial isolationism, and took a Palmerstonian line on the Russian danger in 1853. But he criticized Palmerston for his populist Liberalism, which had alienated continental leaders from Britain and encouraged disruptive nationalist sentiment in Italy. And after the spring of 1855 he became as critical of Palmerston's Crimean War policy as was politically sensible, by tentatively advocating an honourable peace and opposing the notion of an ideologically inspired extension to the war aimed at reshaping Europe in a liberal direction. As a result, in 1855–6, as at other times in the 1850s, many Conservatives felt that he was too ineffective against Palmerston, out of touch with popular patriotic sentiment, and too closely associated with some radicals.

Disraeli's third sphere of concern was the inadequacy of British rule in India. In 1853 he opposed the renewal of the East India Company's charter on the grounds that its government was weak and careless; it had failed to provide effective finance, justice, public works, or education. 'Clear and complete responsibility' was needed and was badly lacking; if the Commons failed to insist on a searching inquiry in preparation for firm and just rule, it would lose India (*Hansard 3*, 128, 1853, 1032). These arguments were too close to those of radical India reformers for the taste of many Conservatives, who wished to uphold the traditional ties between the East India Company and the party. Disraeli further alarmed party opinion by his response to the 1857 Indian mutiny, when he disparaged the vindictiveness, racism, and misrepresentations of the British media. (He was particularly amused by the consequences of the report that thirteen British ladies had had their noses cut off by the rebels, which had generated outraged cant from Lord Shaftesbury and an offer by a surgeon to supply artificial noses if the taxpayer would foot the bill.)

Rather than meeting 'atrocities by atrocities', Disraeli called for a more philosophical approach by British rulers (Monypenny and Buckle, 4.99). Since 1848 British policy had taken a new and foolish path, alienating Hindu and Muslim alike by a lack of respect for native religions, a contempt for traditional property rights, and an ignorance of other laws and customs. The Indians had been goaded to do what in 1853 he had thought impossible: to sink their differences against the British. Disraeli urged, among other things, a greater symbolic role for the queen as a comprehensible, godlike embodiment of British interest and authority capable of engaging the oriental imagination. She should pledge to respect 'their laws, their usages, their customs, and above all their religion' (*Hansard 3*, 147, 479). He attacked Palmerston's proposals of 1858 for Indian government on the ground that they involved another quick fix, in this case an entirely nominated council, selected by the home government, to advise the governor-general. A nominated body, reminiscent of late eighteenth-century corruption, would be unaccountable to parliament and unable to check the governor-general's despotism. A royal commission, sent out to India, was needed to investigate the practical failings of government and maximize its revenues. Palmerston fell and the new minority Conservative government had to

settle the immediate question and to accept the
principle of a council. Disraeli proposed 'a real
Council', with half its members directly elected,
five by the electors of major British towns, but
the Liberal majority in parliament forced the
government to remodel the bill on more conventional lines. The India issue demonstrated
how Disraeli could be a committed supporter
of empire, yet be distrusted for both his radical reformism and his distaste for populist chauvinism.

The fourth issue was parliamentary reform. Disraeli's quixotic proposals for colonial representation demonstrated a willingness to experiment
with the electoral system in order to consolidate
the empire. In 1848 he had criticized the whig
reformers of 1832 for their narrowness and ahis-
toricism in introducing a rigid property qualifica-
tion for the borough franchise, while disparaging
the factitious reopening of the question until
there was a prospect of settling it (*Hansard 3*, 99,
1848, 952). Once Lord John Russell had placed
parliamentary reform on the agenda again, Disraeli saw that a blustering Conservative response
risked uniting their opponents in favour of a
bill, and leaving themselves typecast, as in 1832,

as unthinking opponents of reform. Equally, the longer the issue remained unsettled, the more scope there would be for dangerous agitation in support of radical ends such as a major redistribution of seats, diminishing the number of MPs who would represent the 'realised experience of a nation' (ibid., 956). So it was sensible for the government of 1858–9 to attempt to settle the question, especially given the scope for party advantage in the detailed terms, and the momentum that a minority government would gain by carrying a prestigious bill. However, the proposals could not afford to upset Conservative MPs in case they formed an anti-reform cave in alliance with Palmerston. So the 1859 Reform Bill concentrated on equalizing the county and borough franchise. This conceded the principle of a lower county franchise to radicals who had campaigned for it, while crucially allowing the government to propose the exclusion of (largely Liberal) borough freeholders from the county constituencies, thus preserving their historic identity. But the government's failure to agree on any safe and definitive reduction of the borough franchise ensured the bill's defeat by Liberal MPs. Ministers dissolved parliament after the defeat, and gained seats at the 1859 election.

In the 1850s Disraeli also spent much energy on disseminating these and other Conservative ideas in *The Press*, a weekly journal founded in 1853 on his initiative and that of Derby's son Lord Stanley, his close ally in these years. Disraeli conceived of this as a modern *Anti-Jacobin*, engaged in an urgent war of ideas with an overwhelmingly and previously unchallenged Liberal press. It was tolerably successful, with a circulation of over 3000 at its best. Disraeli and Stanley wrote many articles for it, as did some able young journalists; in the case of the second editor, D. T. Coulton (1854–7), it is known that Disraeli dictated a policy to him at the Commons each week (Kebbel, 3–4). Many Conservatives were annoyed at the way in which Disraeli used the journal to expound his opinions, and he severed his connection with it on taking office in 1858.

The Press was merely one of the ways in which Disraeli sought to enhance the standing of the party in the 1850s. He took an active interest in the overhaul of party organization, and appointed his solicitor Philip Rose to handle it in 1853; Markham Spofforth, a member of Rose's firm, succeeded him as agent between 1859 and 1870. Yet the party could not break through to gain a majority, even in 1859. Nor could the government win supporters from outside Conservative ranks, though William Gladstone and Sir James Graham were approached to join the cabinet in 1858. (Disraeli was willing to surrender the leadership of the Commons to the latter but not the former.) Disraeli also made various attempts to woo independent whig, radical, and Irish MPs in the last desperate days of the ministry in 1859. These failed, as did the attempt to persuade Palmerston to join the government. As a result, it was defeated in parliament on the question of Italy in June 1859. Disraeli was out of office once again. He had a pension of £2000 p.a.—and praise from the political commentator Walter Bagehot, who argued that he alone had kept the government in power for sixteen months and that he had learned (unlike in 1852) to 'lead with dignity, and fail with dignity' (*Historical Essays*, 485).

Opposition, 1859–1865: church defence

Disraeli knew that it would be impossible to persuade enough Conservative MPs to mount a full-scale opposition to a reassuringly quietist Palmerston government. By manoeuvring against it, he would be forced into alliances that they found distasteful, which would further weaken his own position. His 'shameless' past tendencies in this direction were bitterly criticized in an anonymous article in the *Quarterly Review* in April 1860 (written, as was quickly well known, by Lord Robert Cecil, the future marquess of Salisbury). Depressed, he offered to resign the Commons leadership in a letter to an influential senior back-bencher, Sir William Miles, written in June. This had the predictable effect of rallying support to him. But Disraeli learned his lesson and made few controversial initiatives during the next five sessions. Parliamentary reform was a dormant issue, while there was little scope to unite the party in criticism of government finance.

Disraeli's main activity between 1861 and 1865 was on an issue on which he could develop his ideas while satisfying most Conservative prejudices and perhaps making common ground with Irish Catholic MPs: church defence. The abolition of church rates was one of the few principles on which Palmerston was willing to court advanced Liberal opinion, and in reaction the Conservatives were able to defend the rate successfully in divisions in 1861, 1862, and 1863. Disraeli, not previously a clerical politician, identified a 'real Church party in the House of Commons' for the first time in twenty years (Monypenny and Buckle, 4.291), and became interested in the wider potential of the issue. He held discussions with Bishop Wilberforce and addressed gatherings in the cause outside parliament. The most famous took place at Oxford in November 1864, when he asserted that the root question between the evolutionists and the church was, 'Is man an ape or an angel?', and declared himself 'on the side of the angels' (ibid., 374). Disraeli's epigrammatic and idiosyncratic language on religious matters was mocked by opponents and offensive to grave churchmen. He in turn criticized the factionalism of the high-church ritualists, a 'finical and fastidious crew' who were as corrosively subversive of church power as the radical dissenters (ibid., 358) and whose ceremonial symbolized doctrines that the church had been established in order to repudiate (*Letters...to Lady Bradford and Lady Chesterfield*, 1.156). He made some serious proposals for greater lay involvement in church life and politics, maintaining that exclusive clericalism was damaging the church's ability to engage on a broad basis with the national imagination and to regain its position as the natural, safe, and patriotic depository of man's age-old religious instincts.

Arguably that position was occupied by the
Catholic church in most of Ireland, and by the
papacy in its own dominions, hence Disraeli's
fascination with the power of Catholicism. In the
1860s he sought to court Irish Catholic MPs at the
same time as he upheld the Church of England.
Indeed the successful Commons defence of church
rates was assisted by the abstention of some
Irish Catholic MPs, while a significant number
of Irishmen supported the opposition's censure
motion on Palmerston's foreign policy in 1864.
Disraeli claimed to defend religion on an international basis against the modern decaying principles of republicanism and atheism. He upheld
the temporal power of the pope—'an old man
on a Semitic throne' (Disraeli, *Bentinck*, 509)—
against its circling opponents. At one stage he
was alarmed that Napoleon III, mishandled by
the British government, might incite nationalist
and revolutionary movements against the papacy.
Almost alone of major British politicians, Disraeli
refused to meet the Italian patriot Garibaldi on his
visit of 1864. He thought that the religious principles of Irish Catholics should make them natural
Conservatives. A shared defence of religion was
also the only way of forming an alliance with
the numerous group of Irish MPs without surren-
dering to separatist or anti-landlord principles.

The Reform drama and the premiership

4

Prelude to power

By the time of the 1865 election Disraeli had gained in position. The Conservatives, though still in a minority, won 290 seats at that election, and would doubtless have won more but for the popularity of Palmerston. Disraeli had become a more familiar figure in establishment circles, especially at court, where his ability to pay lavish public respect to the memory of Prince Albert won the queen's affection even more than his willingness to refrain from attempting to unseat her government. He was excited beyond measure by his reception there, particularly by a much coveted invitation to the wedding of the prince of Wales in 1863 (shrewdly arranged by Palmerston). In 1865 he was at last made a member of Grillion's, a socially select political dining club, and in 1866 of the Athenaeum, from which he had been blackballed in 1832. It was also now that he could finally put his debts behind him, owing to two strokes of financial good fortune. In 1862 Andrew Montagu, a landed Yorkshire bachelor who wished to assist the party, bought up Disraeli's debts in return for offering him a £57,000 mortgage on Hughenden, charging a rate of interest only 30 per cent of that asked by his previous creditors. In 1863 Disraeli inherited over £30,000 from Mrs Sarah Brydges Willyams, an aged Jewish lady of Torquay with whom he had struck up a close friendship in the early 1850s. He and she were united in the belief that they were descended from aristocratic Jewish Iberian houses, and Mrs Brydges Willyams's legacy— given in 'approbation and admiration of his efforts to vindicate the race of Israel' (Monypenny and Buckle, 3.466)—was accompanied by the hope that he would adopt the names and arms of the two families concerned, though fortunately this was not a condition of the bequest. She was buried at Hughenden (which she never visited), with the Disraelis beside her.

Despite these advances, Disraeli was not much nearer power, and was frequently lethargic and depressed at this time. He was over sixty, still widely distrusted personally, and a leading member of a party that could neither win elections on its own nor attract parliamentary support from other potentially sympathetic factions. In this situation the death of Palmerston in October 1865 was both an opportunity and a danger. It made the radical forces in the Liberal coalition more undisciplined; it encouraged Lord John Russell and Gladstone to court them by resuscitating the issue of parliamentary reform. It was fairly clear that this initiative would restore a vigorous two-party system and allow a proper battle between conservatism and radicalism. It was far less clear that the Conservative Party would be able to dictate the tactics of the first of these two forces. This was evident from the events generated by the 1866 Reform Bill, which was staunchly opposed by a faction of anti-democratic Liberals, the Adullamites, who eventually defeated it in alliance with the Conservatives in June 1866 and forced Russell's Liberal government out of office. The Adullamites then demanded a coalition with the Conservatives in which Derby and Disraeli should surrender the leading places to more centrist figures. Derby and Disraeli rejected this offer and formed a purely Conservative government, with Disraeli once again chancellor of the exchequer and leader of the Commons. In doing so, they were attempting to keep alive not only their own careers but also the Conservative Party. That remained their first objective throughout the following eighteen turbulent months, and does much to explain the history of the second Reform Act.

The Reform Act of 1867

The history of the reform question, and of previous minority Conservative governments, held a number of crucial lessons for the new ministers. First, they had to consolidate their reputation as reformers by bringing in a bill—a fact that became all the clearer as extra-parliamentary agitation, exploited by radicals, developed during the months after the Liberal defeat. Second, they had to satisfy urban agitators by lowering the borough franchise, which they had been condemned for not doing in 1859; they might mitigate the radical effects of this by establishing a principle broad enough to settle the question for a generation. Third, their proposals had to benefit the Conservatives electorally and uphold the territorial element within the constitution, by ridding the county constituencies of as many Liberal urban and suburban voters as possible. Fourth, they needed to establish a definite parliamentary identity which could keep the party in charge of the political situation and avoid an enforced subordination to Liberals and Adullamites that might last for years. Fifth, they could do this only by exploiting splits in the Liberal Party that would prevent it from asserting its natural majority. None of this need involve a breach of principle.

The events that resulted in the 1867 Reform Act followed naturally from those points. Disraeli hoped originally to avoid introducing a bill in the 1867 session, and to proceed by resolutions instead, with the aim of establishing some sort of consensus; however, that was too unpopular in the Commons. It was decided to base the government proposal on the principle of household suffrage in the boroughs for those who paid rates personally (accompanied by qualifications such as a two-year residence requirement and various 'fancy franchises'). This was popular among Conservative MPs, politically attractive, and potentially capable of providing a defensible long-term resting place. When a minority in cabinet dissented, and forced the government to propose a more limited bill, large numbers of MPs on both sides disliked that idea and, in March, forced the ministry back on household suffrage, a decision that Derby and Disraeli welcomed (though it led to the resignation of three cabinet ministers, led by Robert Cecil, who had become Lord Cranborne). A bill constructed on this basis, with the threat of a dissolution if it was defeated, placed the Liberal leadership in an awkward position. Disraeli exploited this effectively throughout the 1867 session, dividing Gladstone from radical MPs and showing up many Liberals as much less wholehearted reformers than their self-presentation as champions of 'the people' had suggested. A crucial influence on the outcome was that the main qualifications to household suffrage in the original bill did not survive the process of amendment in committee, because they were inconsistent with existing electoral practice or politically unattractive to a majority of the Commons. Disraeli accepted amendments when he considered them necessary to get the bill through, including, most importantly, the amendment proposed by Grosvenor Hodgkinson in mid-May, abolishing compounding. This increased substantially the numbers paying rates personally, with consequent effects for the size of the borough electorate (though it was generally assumed that many of those affected would not register). He refused to accept amendments proposed by Gladstone, in order to underline his loss of control over both wings of his party. Liberal discomfiture assisted Conservative support for Disraeli throughout the session, indeed made him generally popular on the back benches. Most Conservatives, including Disraeli, had no precise sense of the consequences of the bill for the borough electorate, but these were in any case almost impossible to predict. The essence of the matter was that the Liberals would continue to dominate in the large boroughs most affected by the bill, while the lack of large-scale redistribution prevented the destruction of traditional interest representation. The redistribution arrangements also altered some county boundaries so as to reinforce their rural and Conservative nature. One estimate suggests that the Liberal majority was reduced by twenty-five seats at the 1868 election as a result (Cowling, *1867*, 344–5).

The passage of the 1867 Reform Act added to the distrust of Disraeli felt by his critics in the party, most vehement among them Lord Cranborne (later Lord Salisbury). Elsewhere, however, it increased his reputation. The act had strengthened the government's hold over the Commons, given it a legislative success in the country, settled a difficult question quickly (to the pleasure, among others, of the queen), and made it impossible for Liberals to sustain their claim to a monopoly of electoral progressivism. It introduced a more democratic political era in which the most fundamental division would clearly be between conservatism and radicalism, but it destroyed the schemes of political reconstruction that might have prevented the Conservative Party from reaping the benefit of any Conservative reaction. Disraeli's tactical skill and courage in steering a bill through the Commons with a majority of seventy against him was remarkable, though he was by no means master of the situation, and his broad strategy was similar to that of many shrewd Conservatives. None the less the drama contributed to the myth of him as a mysterious, aloof manipulator, and consolidated both positive and negative sides of his public image. It made it even easier than before for his enemies to question his principles, but it also ensured that, when Derby's gout became so bad that he was forced to resign the premiership in February 1868, the queen turned to Disraeli to continue the government. He kissed hands at Osborne House on 27 February, declaring 'In loving loyalty & faith' (Blake, 491).

Little opposition to Disraeli's appointment was expressed within the party. However, he was hardly in a position to develop a new line of policy, even had he wanted to do so. He made little change to the cabinet. Having long been Derby's Commons manager, he seemed very anxious to continue to seek his protection; he consulted him frequently and in his election address of October 1868 wrote that he had carried out Derby's policy 'without deviation' (Monypenny and Buckle, 5.88). It was ironic that on expenditure, the issue on which he and Derby had most frequently failed to see eye to eye, Disraeli was not able to implement tax reductions: income tax, $4d.$ in 1866, had to rise from $5d.$ to $6d.$ in 1868. Disraeli had finally succeeded in checking Conservative tendencies to increase defence expenditure, only to have to meet the bill for the Abyssinian expedition of 1867–8. The expedition was forced on the government, and certainly not undertaken for electoral popularity, but Disraeli none the less used its successful conclusion to make a point to commercial public opinion, the isolationism of which was beginning to irritate him. In two speeches he suggested that in an age accused, 'perhaps not unjustly, of selfishness, and a too great regard for material interests', it was a legitimate source of pride to have 'elevated the military' and 'moral ... character of England throughout the world' (*Selected Speeches*, 2.132; *The Times*, 18 June 1868, 9) .

Disraeli's first premiership was dominated by Ireland, but this was not his doing. Derby had controlled the government's Irish policy, together with the Irish secretary, Lord Mayo. They aimed to conciliate moderate Catholics without alienating protestant feeling by any major concession on the status of the Church of Ireland. Negotiations had taken place with the Irish hierarchy and Henry Manning, archbishop of Westminster, about the possible grant of a charter to a Catholic university. On 10 March, Mayo announced this policy, which met with a lukewarm response from the Catholic bishops, who sought amendments. He proposed a small endowment for university expenses, and left open the larger issue of endowment for the denominational teaching colleges. Six days later Gladstone declared that an endowed university was a political impossibility and soon proposed the disestablishment and disendowment of the Irish church. This initiative united whig and radical wings of the Liberal Party, attracted Irish Catholic MPs away from the government, played to evangelical British protestants' visceral hatred of Catholic endowment, and placed the Conservative Party in the position of having to defend an institution which few British voters admired. Whatever other motives Gladstone had for this move, the desire to remove Disraeli from the highest office was widely assumed to be one of them. The future of the Irish church became the major question at the general election of November 1868. In speech after speech Gladstone ruthlessly charged Disraeli with favouring a policy of Catholic endowment, which he had not been able to persuade his party to support. Conservatives were indeed divided on an Irish church policy, and scarcely able to counter-attack.

The election was delayed until fresh registers, including the new electors, were ready. This allowed Disraeli to cling to office, despite the indignity of several crucial defeats on the Irish church issue in April and May. He had little knowledge of electoral opinion nationwide, but county agents' reports suggested hostility to Catholic and high Anglican practices, and this confirmed his decision to base his campaign around the church defence policy that he had been maturing earlier in the decade. He accused

Romanists and ritualists of forming an open confederacy in favour of disestablishment, from which each hoped to benefit. However, Disraeli's campaign was low-key; he made only one speech, on re-election to his seat, after most of the contests had been decided. Instead, he sought to use the church patronage that fell to him to rally evangelical protestant sentiment, by making the fiery Liverpool preacher Hugh McNeile dean of Ripon in an obvious bid for their votes. He also rejected the leading high-church candidate for the bishopric of London, Samuel Wilberforce. Disraeli did not seek to alienate traditional high-churchmen, and in fact made several low-key appointments from that party. Moreover, he was not sufficiently well informed about candidates for promotion to be able to dominate church patronage (he had to give way to the queen, for example, over the appointment of the new archbishop of Canterbury, A. C. Tait). His strategy of rallying churchmen to the party achieved little, partly because of the tension between church factions and between representatives of those factions in his own party. In any case, more important in explaining the election result was the attraction of Gladstone's policy to many evangelical dissenters and Celtic voters. The Liberals nearly doubled their majority, to 110 seats, and Disraeli resigned on 1 December 1868, without meeting parliament: a constitutional innovation that was generally approved in the circumstances. The queen granted his request to confer the title of Viscountess Beaconsfield on his wife.

Defeat and bereavement

The defection of the Irish Catholics ended Disraeli's dream of combining them with Anglicans in defence of the Semitic religious legacy. He reflected on this in the light of stirring contemporary events outside Britain: the unification of Italy (and in particular the struggle for control of Rome), the papal declarations that culminated in the Vatican Council, the resurgence of the American republic in 1865, the emergence of the First International, and developments in biblical criticism and scientific materialism. To him all seemed evidence of an immense conflict between faith and ecclesiastical organization on the one hand, and free thought, republicanism, and secular nationalism on the other.

This 'death struggle' was the theme of *Lothair*, the novel that—to general astonishment—Disraeli produced secretly for publication in May 1870. Lothair—another Tancred—is a young English aristocrat, heir to fabulous wealth, whose affections are engaged alternately by three charismatic young women, representing respectively his own caste, the Catholic church, and the secret societies (which Disraeli, true to his Romantic individualism, persisted in seeing as the fount of international radical agitation). Disraeli portrays the appeal of each value system with unmistakable affection; a part of him could see how each could appeal to a noble youth of ambition, and indeed the title-page quotation suggested that it was salutary for young men to experiment with them all. Catholicism offers tradition, a mother figure, imposing ceremonial, and an unshakeable faith with which to combat modern doubts and luxury. The various secular ideals described in the book are similarly hostile to contemporary selfish materialism and celebrate freedom of conscience, humanity, and the beauty of nature. The English landowning ideal reverences order, hierarchy, patriotism, and public service. None the less, Disraeli's intention is to show that the continent's two warring principles are flawed owing to their infidelity to the Semitic legacy. The Roman church is based on too narrow and conciliar a

obvious successor, Stanley, who succeeded as fifteenth earl of Derby on his father's death in 1869, even refused the leadership in the Lords in 1870, because he did not like to handle such a clerical party and preferred to be an *éminence grise* steering it towards the middle ground.

However, a change of political climate in the early 1870s went some way to justifying the forebodings expressed in *Lothair*. The Vatican Council and the *Kulturkampf* on the one hand, the fall of Rome and the Paris commune on the other, imparted a new intensity to the struggle between the papacy and secular nationalism, and brought home to Englishmen the disturbing foreignness of both ideals. Meanwhile the rapid outcome of the Franco-Prussian War, the unification of Germany, the Russian abrogation of the neutralization of the Black Sea, and the indignity of the Alabama claims settlement alarmed a domestic public opinion nurtured on Palmerstonian and free-trading confidence in Britain's global position. In such circumstances, the self-effacement of British foreign policy seemed weak and dangerous, while the government's concessionary Irish policy, the Liberal Party's republican fringe, and the radical demands for disestablishment and secular education could be presented as indications of Gladstonian unsoundness in the impending battle for the maintenance of the nation's institutions, religious establishments, property, and world influence. These themes badly damaged Gladstone's government. Conservatives needed no leading to press these points home, and Disraeli's contribution to the collapse of Liberal popularity was small. However, a major theme of the two extra-parliamentary speeches that he made in 1872, at Manchester and the Crystal Palace, was that England faced a crucial choice: whether to play a responsible world role befitting her imperial status, or to decay under the spell of cosmopolitan principles. The most important decision he took in these years was a strategic parliamentary one, not to take office in a minority when Gladstone's Irish University Bill was defeated in March 1873, but to wait for an enfeebled Liberal Party to dissolve parliament.

Disraeli's second premiership, 1874–1880

Competent, sober government

Despite Liberal weaknesses, at the beginning of 1874 there was little reason to expect a rapid return to power. In fact, Disraeli was prime minister again before the beginning of the session, owing to Gladstone's unexpected dissolution and decisive defeat at the election. The Conservatives had over 350 seats. Disraeli took office on 18 February. At last he had achieved his great ambition, power with a majority—something that had seemed impossible for most of his life. He certainly took pleasure in the position. He enjoyed the process of dispensing patronage, especially to deserving old connections, and was amused by the number of beseeching letters that he received. Patronage was very valuable for a party so long in opposition, and he asserted his right to appoint to a number of posts that the Treasury had tried to depoliticize. From now until his death he enjoyed a close proximity to Queen Victoria, to whom he reported political and social news with irreverent gusto; in 1868, for example, he had commented to her of his colleague Ward Hunt that, 'like St. Peter's no one is aware of his dimensions. But he has the sagacity of an elephant as well as the form' (Blake, 488–9). She responded with obvious marks of favour to him (including allowing him to sit during audiences), though he found her excessively demanding—and sometimes 'very mad' (*Selection from the Diaries of…Derby*, 290)—and he needed all his tact to deal with her and especially with the affairs of the prince of Wales.

Disraeli was a ceremonious, slightly remote, but patient and unassertive chairman of cabinet, which conducted its business with laxity. Its priorities were broadly agreed. On the one hand, it stood for the principle of 'not harassing the country' (Mitchell, 61), and was dominated by landowners and high-churchmen anxious to prevent assaults on property and religious institutions. Most formidable of these was Salisbury, who now returned to office. On the other, it reflected the great opportunity that the party had to become a centrist force, offering competent, sober government as uncontroversially as possible, leaving undisturbed the fiscal basis of mid-Victorian England, and offering the Liberals little chance of recovering the middle ground. This was the strategy associated particularly with Derby, and with R. A. Cross, the 'middle-class' Lancashire man brought in as home secretary at Derby's prompting, despite Disraeli's 'odd dislike' of men of that class (*Selection from the Diaries of … Derby*, 416). Fiscal rectitude was signalled by the appointment as chancellor of the exchequer of Stafford Northcote, Disraeli's protégé but also Gladstone's. The cabinet was reduced to twelve members, the smallest since 1832, to indicate the importance of efficiency, economy, and individual responsibility in government.

Disraeli's election address had reverted to the theme of *Lothair*, the need to maintain England's influence as the defender of civil and religious liberty against the threat from Catholicism and atheism. In the 1874 session he capitalized on this protestant cry in such a way as to ensure that the Liberals remained split and listless. (He unsuccessfully offered one whig dissident, the duke of

Somerset, cabinet office in 1874 and again in 1878.) 'I detest and disagree' with the Irish MPs, he told Henry Ponsonby, the queen's private secretary (Monypenny and Buckle, 5.211). But especially now that so many had declared for home rule, Disraeli needed to do little in that direction except to oppose the home rule idea staunchly. He exploited divisions in the Liberals most effectively by his handling of the Public Worship Regulation Bill, urged on the government by Archbishop Tait in order to provide the bishops with a way of disciplining ritualist excesses in parishes. Protestant feeling for such a measure was very strong, and some action was politically necessary. The government improved Tait's bill behind the scenes, but by delaying official support for it Disraeli kept the clerical factions in his cabinet united. When Gladstone opposed it, opening a rift with most of his party, he finally supported it and was influential in the subsequent compromise which carried the bill. He thus achieved the dual objective of damaging Gladstone (who subsequently retired as Liberal leader) and of settling a question that had the potential to antagonize all church parties. The church, he wrote, 'will be immensely strengthened' by the disciplining of such a controversial minority (ibid.,

5.322), though the act itself was to cause tension inside the Anglican body. Another government act of 1874 abolished patronage in the Church of Scotland, in the hope of reducing the threat of a disestablishment agitation there. This terminated Disraeli's active involvement with church issues. Though they were very contentious in the 1870s, producing further squabbles between clerical factions within the party, these were kept in check.

The strategy of concentrating on bipartisan social issues was developed by Cross and Derby in association with Disraeli in 1874 and matured in the six substantial bills passed in the 1875 session, which were intended to make an effective contrast with the Liberals' destructive hyper-activity. This was a strategy particularly attractive to the hard-headed practical Conservatism of northern MPs, and Disraeli was well advised to insert two paragraphs on sanitary reform in the long speech that he had been persuaded to make at Manchester in 1872. They bestowed extravagant praise on the 'practical' scheme to consolidate sanitary legislation then being proposed by his colleague Sir Charles Adderley. He accompanied this praise with a conventional warning against abstractions, against dreamily trusting too much to the state in social affairs rather than to private effort (*Selected Speeches*, 2.510–11). That these paragraphs later spawned the exceptionally long-lived myth of Disraeli as social reformer is a great historical curiosity. In government Disraeli left his departmental heads to produce their own legislation and was no man for detail; indeed Derby felt that one of his shortcomings as cabinet chairman was that he 'detests the class of business which he is apt to call parochial' (*Selection from the Diaries of ... Derby*, 448). He did not mention his government's social measures in his only intervention at the 1880 election. What he especially valued in the legislation of 1875 was that by settling difficult questions it reduced the 'materials for social agitation' (Mitchell, 89). This was so particularly of the labour laws legislation and the Agricultural Holdings Act, which he saw as checking ill feeling between employers and employees and between landlords and farmers. In the financial sphere the large surplus inherited in 1874 made it easy to agree a policy for the first budget. Northcote pleased all the major interest groups by relieving the three categories of direct, indirect, and local taxation; income tax fell to 2*d*.

In the 1874 session and the first half of the next Disraeli was widely agreed to be in command of the Commons, demonstrating an 'easy confidence', a 'polite consideration' for MPs, and a refusal to cajole or hurry them (Lucy, 39, 46, 68, 82). However, his powers then seemed to wane. He was often ill—with gout, asthma, and bronchitis—and tired: he once fell asleep in cabinet in 1875. In 1876 he had to encounter persistent Liberal factionalism over the Royal Titles Bill, and the beginnings of obstruction from the home-rulers. The Conservative back-benchers were restive at the lack of achievement in the session. Despite having the 'most numerous and obedient majority since Pitt', he seemed unable to dispatch routine matters at ordinary times. That he lacked facility for business became apparent: 'an incessant and almost avowed inaccuracy pervades him' (*Historical Essays*, 503). He perceived that his physical powers were not sufficient to continue to lead the Commons effectively. Though he volunteered to resign the premiership, neither he nor his colleagues seriously considered this step. In August 1876 the queen made him earl of Beaconsfield and from the session of 1877 he led the ministry from the Lords.

In 1877 Derby, the sceptical and peace-loving foreign secretary, noted that one reason for the unbusinesslike habits of the cabinet was that Beaconsfield 'takes peculiar pleasure in turning over & discussing all sorts of foreign questions, on which action is not necessary, & often not possible' (*Selection from the Diaries of…Derby*, 448). International issues excited the premier in a way that most others did not: 'these are politics worth managing', he wrote in 1876 (Monypenny and Buckle, 6.32). This was not just because of the attractions of continental intrigue. In 1871 he had hoped that public interest in foreign affairs might divert attention from the 'morbid spirit of domestic change and criticism' (ibid., 5.132). In 1875 he wondered whether the spirit of patriotism was dead or whether it could be rekindled. The attempt to do so became a—perhaps the—major goal of his government.

However, an additional obstacle facing a spirited British policy was that German unification and the fall of France in 1870 had destroyed the European balance and forced Russia, Austria, and Germany to try to settle international questions by mutual agreement for fear of the alternative. Disraeli did not set much store by the French in their enfeebled state, and sought a good understanding with the German chancellor Bismarck, in accordance with his protestant declarations at the 1874 election. However, the war scare of May 1875 showed the impossibility of relying on Bismarck's goodwill, and the British participation in the protest against his threatening behaviour reassured the French. This paid important dividends in November, when news came of the wish of the khedive of Egypt to sell his large minority stake in the Suez Canal Company to French businessmen, thus making it entirely French-owned. The cabinet agreed on the importance of the British securing some stake, and the shares were bought without diplomatic awkwardness, with the assistance of a loan from the Rothschilds arranged by Disraeli (on extravagantly generous terms). Though the company had no control over the canal, and the shares were mortgaged and so had no voting rights, the impression was given that Britain had bought a controlling stake in the canal itself. The general public enthusiasm for this step was an encouraging sign of the popularity of an active international policy.

When, in 1875, revolts began in the Balkans against Turkish rule, Disraeli suggested that the need of Russia, Austria, and Germany to work together to settle the Balkan question threatened to 'drive the Turk from Europe' (Monypenny and Buckle, 6.13). Always susceptible to racial interpretations of history, he feared that Russia would incite pan-Slav sentiment in what he later called a war of 'extermination directed equally against a religion and a race' (*Selection from the Diaries of…Derby*, 442). Secret societies, he claimed, were operating in Serbia and elsewhere to stir up pan-Slav spirit, and this would end in a war that might have revolutionary implications. European Turkey would be partitioned into Russian and Austrian spheres, and Germany would seek compensation elsewhere, perhaps to the west, which would leave France, Belgium, and Britain in a disastrously weakened state. These sweeping notions made Disraeli suspicious of the early attempts by the three eastern powers to seek a limited settlement of the Balkan question; he feared that popular pressure would force the Russian and Austro-Hungarian governments into a partition of European Turkey. As a result, he wished to reject the Andrassy note (which demanded that the Ottoman empire should reform its European administration), which the three powers agreed and sent to Britain for support in December 1875.

It was not easy for the British government to find an alternative to this policy, and Derby secured the acceptance of the note. However, when war between Serbia and Turkey seemed likely in May 1876, Disraeli and Derby agreed to reject a further communication from the three powers, the Berlin memorandum, which sought to pre-empt war by warning of great-power intervention in the Ottoman empire if reforms were not carried out. The British asserted instead the importance of the powers upholding the old treaty policy of guaranteeing the integrity and independence of the Ottoman empire. This was essentially an attempt to buy time for a better policy. Indeed, the government tried unsuccessfully to reach a settlement with Russia in June 1876 that would not only assert British influence in the region but, while revising Ottoman frontiers, would also avert a general partition.

At this point news reached Britain of Turkish massacres of Bulgarian Christians in response to an uprising. This prompted a prolonged and virtuous agitation at home, into which Gladstone entered with relish. The Bulgarian agitation had three effects on the prime minister. First, he believed that it made Russia more likely to go to war against Turkey, with pan-Slavism aroused and sympathy for the Balkan Christians so strong in the British public that the British government could not object. Second, it delivered another and perhaps the greatest blow to his reputation with Liberal opinion, because he proclaimed his suspicion that many of the sensational details published in the newspapers were inventions of Slavonic intriguers. His remarks were seen as callous and flippant. Indeed in September 1876 he was famously and disastrously misunderstood when he described Gladstone's pamphlet on the atrocities as likely to cause 'general havoc and ruin' in the Balkans (by encouraging war) and thus 'worse than any of those Bulgarian atrocities which now occupy attention' (*The Times*, 21 Sept 1876, 6). Third, it added to internal Conservative Party pressure for a change of policy, particularly from the section of high-churchmen led by Salisbury who sympathized with the persecuted Orthodox Christians.

Neither Beaconsfield nor Derby believed it very likely that Russia could be stopped from declaring war on Turkey. However, Derby proposed an international conference at Constantinople in an attempt to reach agreement on increased self-government for parts of European Turkey, and the government sent Salisbury as its representative in an effort to show British and continental opinion that it was amenable to reform. The Turks resisted the conference proposals, as expected, and despite further attempts at a settlement, the Russians prepared for war in the spring of 1877; they declared it in late April.

Assertion in the Near East

Until this point Beaconsfield had generally followed the policy laid down by Derby, though he embellished it with a few characteristically restless but fruitless initiatives and a general desire to make an impression in Europe. The Russian invasion of European Turkey changed the situation because the ultimate threat was now to Constantinople and thus to British interests in the eastern Mediterranean, Egypt, and Asia. The immediate consequence was a deeply damaging split in the Liberal opposition, which benefited the government temporarily. However, Beaconsfield was extremely aware of the disaster that would strike any government that appeared lax in safeguarding British interests. He was haunted by the experience of 1853 and the obloquy earned by Aberdeen's government for failing to prevent the Crimean War. Old and ill as he was, this was not how he wished to be remembered by posterity. From now until January 1878 cabinet politics were dominated by various attempts made by him to counter the Russian advance, all of which were frustrated by Derby and (usually) a majority of the cabinet. The situation was worsened by the Turkish resistance at Plevna from July to December 1877, which delayed the dénouement. At various times Beaconsfield proposed to occupy the Gallipoli peninsula, with or without the sultan's permission (which was not given). However, this required money from parliament, for which he shrank from asking. It was also likely to offend the powers on whose goodwill Derby thought Britain depended in order to achieve a settlement of the crisis. Derby and some other ministers believed that the Russians' goals were moderate, that they would not occupy Constantinople permanently even if they entered it, and that the weight of European pressure on them would then ensure a fair solution. Derby (who was seen in cabinet as at least as plausible an interpreter of middle-class sentiment as Beaconsfield) also argued that, with trade worsening, there was little pro-war feeling in the country. Salisbury at this stage was similarly averse to strong measures. In an attempt to explain the absence of action Beaconsfield, continually harassed by the belligerent Victoria, traduced both these colleagues in letters to her. For many years these letters provided the main version of cabinet discussions and still influence many accounts, but it is now clear, from Derby's diary, that the cabinet as a whole was in charge of policy and able to rationalize it.

However, the situation was altered in December 1877 by the fall of Plevna and the impending return of parliament. The first of these excited both the Conservative press, with which Beaconsfield's private secretary Montagu Corry was in daily contact, and the queen, who visited Hughenden on 15 December in order to show her support for her prime minister against his critics. Political society and the press became aware of splits in the cabinet. The balance within the cabinet was affected by the threat to British interests and by the imminence of the parliamentary session; Salisbury in particular became much more sympathetic to Beaconsfield's position. On 23 January 1878, with Russia menacing Constantinople, the cabinet supported Beaconsfield's proposal to send the fleet through the Dardanelles and to ask parliament for a vote of credit. The earls of Carnarvon and of Derby resigned. The fleet was recalled almost immediately, because of reports that the sultan had agreed to peace, together with alarm in the City at the evidence of victory by the war faction in cabinet, and panic within the Conservative Party at the prospect of losing Derby's influence in Lancashire. Derby (but not Carnarvon) thus remained in the cabinet. This crisis lowered respect for the government outside Westminster, generating hostility to further vacillation and a widespread and often bellicose anti-Russian sentiment, christened 'jingoism' after a popular music-hall song. This was accompanied by the spread of ugly rumours about Derby in political society, including the allegation that he or his wife was telling the (surely unsurprised) Russian ambassador of cabinet divisions. These rumours, which Beaconsfield helped to publicize, conveniently disguised the extent of his own covert operations with secret agents and the Rothschilds. The combined effect of these developments was to create a strong climate of opinion within

the party in favour of a policy of resistance to
Russia.

Part of the fleet was sent through the Dardanelles in early February, in response to exaggerated rumours of further Russian advances. This was a popular move at home, though of doubtful strategic value. Had it led to a Russian occupation of Gallipoli and Constantinople, as well it might have, the British were in a vulnerable position. Instead the Russians forced the Turks to sign an objectionable treaty at San Stefano, which at first they seemed unwilling to submit for ratification by the European powers at the congress that Austria now proposed. In response, on 27 March, Beaconsfield persuaded the cabinet to agree to call out the reserves, to bring Indian troops to Malta, and, if Russia was not sufficiently amenable at the congress, to seize the Turkish territory of Cyprus and Iskenderun as British naval bases. (Only the first of these measures was then announced and the third was not necessarily definitely adopted.) This policy had several advantages for him: it satisfied an expectant party, it met the desire of a majority of cabinet that Britain should increase her claim to influence in Asiatic Turkey, and it led to the final resignation of Derby and his replacement as foreign secretary by Salisbury. It also involved little risk, since Germany, Austria, and most Balkan politicians were similarly aggrieved at the treaty of San Stefano and were insistent that Russia must come to the conference table, at Berlin.

Accordingly, Beaconsfield's policy of firmness appeared to lead to a triumphant diplomatic victory almost as soon as it was adopted. Salisbury negotiated a settlement with Russia in advance of the congress at Berlin. This settlement forced her to abandon the idea of a Mediterranean coast for the new Bulgarian state. However, it accepted most of her demands in the Near East; in compensation, Salisbury increased Britain's commitment to the region markedly. He gave the Turks a military alliance, in return for which he forced them to accept British control of Cyprus and the installation of British military consuls in Turkey's Asia Minor territories to guarantee administrative stability and British influence. In cabinet Beaconsfield envisaged that infiltration by British state servants would produce a steady growth of influence in Turkey and Egypt and argued that 'the virtual administration of the East by England was the only hope for the prosperity of those

Countries and Peoples' (Howard and Gordon, 19). The public affirmation of Britain's increased weight in Europe came at the congress of Berlin itself, in June and July, at which Beaconsfield was the most prominent British representative. Despite frequent illness, he revelled in its great set pieces and social events, and the feeling that men of power like himself had assembled to remake the map of Europe. He was fascinated by Bismarck, with whom he enjoyed discussions about the preservation of the aristocratic system with which they both identified so strongly; Bismarck told him that there was no danger of socialism in England as long as upper and working classes were united by a love of horse-racing. On returning from Berlin, Beaconsfield and Salisbury encountered cheering crowds at Dover and Charing Cross, and Beaconsfield made a telling comparison with the failure of 1853 by remarking that he hoped he had brought back peace with honour. The queen offered him a marquessate or dukedom, which he refused; he and Salisbury accepted the Garter.

Beaconsfield believed that the events of 1878 had restored the prestige of England, both abroad and in the eyes of her own people. This was only one aspect of the story. What had started as a tentative and awkward reaction to isolation, and developed into a desperate avoidance of parliamentary humiliation, had ended in a controversial new line of policy, the occupation of Cyprus and the military alliance with Turkey, and a significant heightening of tension with Russia. This new policy instinctively appealed to Beaconsfield and Salisbury, by asserting Britain's power. But her position in the Near East was arguably unsustainable, at least without major extra military commitments at which a subsequent government would probably cavil. Meanwhile, the crisis of 1876–8 had divided opinion at home and had made Beaconsfield a demonic figure to many Liberals, exciting a lot of antisemitic and anti-alien sentiment. He knew only too well that public opinion was fickle and deeply unreliable, and it is unlikely that his policy in the Eastern crisis was driven largely by a search for electoral gain. The cabinet rejected the idea of a premature dissolution in the summer of 1878, as unconstitutional and unpredictable in its consequences, given the state of the economy, which would determine more votes than a foreign triumph. As far as elections were concerned, the major significance of the Eastern crisis was that its divisiveness gave an enormous fillip to party organization on both

sides. Though in the long run the association of
the Conservatives with the national cause was
to benefit the party greatly, in the context of
1878–80 it ended their best chance at an election
by undermining the bipartisan tone with which
they had been wooing 'moderate' opinion. The
crisis destroyed not only Derby's career in the
party but also the centrist strategy for it that he
had been promoting for thirty years.

'Imperialism', 1876–1880

From 1878 until the election of 1880 Gladstone
attacked Beaconsfield for pursuing a vainglorious
policy of territorial aggrandizement, military dis-
play, imperial symbolism, and contempt for parliament, which was inappropriate for a modern
commercial and Christian people. Though much
exaggerated, these charges were effective because
of the variety of evidence that appeared to support
them.

The word 'imperialism' was first applied to British
politics by hostile newspapers during the debates
about the government bill of 1876 to confer on the
queen the title of empress of India. The title was
said to be un-English and particularly resonant

of the tawdry glitter of the regime of Napoleon III. The proposal of the measure also seemed to suggest an unhealthily close political relationship between Disraeli and the queen. The pressure for the bill did indeed stem from her. However, there was no obligation on Disraeli to accept it, and no reason to think that it did not appeal to him as a natural corollary of the suggestions that he had made in 1857 for a more direct, imposing, imaginative, and sympathetic tone to British rule in India. But it was more controversial than he had anticipated; from February to May 1876 it generated strong opposition from Liberal MPs, forcing him to make several parliamentary speeches in its defence.

Disraeli had no strategy for imperial development, and most of the territorial expansion that took place during his ministry was minor and done in order to facilitate the maintenance of order by local British troops. However, he was extremely concerned about the threat to India apparently posed by the Russian advance in central Asia. Even before the outbreak of tension with Russia over the Balkans, he was anxious to secure the north-west frontier. When that tension arose, he and Salisbury toyed with a plan that the Indian army should occupy Afghanistan and rouse the Muslims of central Asia against the Russians. This was extremely impractical, and the only result was to increase the suspicion of Britain entertained by the emir of Afghanistan, Sher Ali. When the Russians sent a mission to Afghanistan in 1878, Edward Bulwer-Lytton, the Indian viceroy, considered it essential to demand a similar privilege for Britain. Bulwer-Lytton, an appointee and admirer of Beaconsfield, sought to emulate his international achievements. Unfortunately, his headstrong and hectoring approach to Sher Ali met with a rebuff, in response to which Britain declared war against him in November 1878. Beaconsfield sought no war: Bulwer-Lytton ignored one set of cabinet instructions, while the cabinet's decision for war was dictated primarily by the first earl of Cranbrook, the Indian secretary, after Beaconsfield had proposed a more moderate course, the temporary occupation of some territory.

None the less, throughout the crisis Beaconsfield regarded the issue of war or peace as secondary to the maintenance of British honour. He consistently urged firmness to assert Britain's ascendancy, and to avoid the impression of vulnerability before the Muslims of Asia, the powers of Europe, and the Conservative opinion of Britain. In November he justified the war in public as facilitating the creation of a more 'scientific' frontier for India against Russia, and reminded his audience that the future of the empire would depend on whether the people of England had 'the courage and determination of their forefathers' (Monypenny and Buckle, 6.393). By early 1879 the war was won, Sher Ali had fled to die, and his son seemed willing to meet all the British demands, including the acceptance of a mission at Kabul. However, the mission was slaughtered in an uprising six weeks after arriving there. To Beaconsfield this was an opportunity to establish the scientific frontier beyond doubt. Kabul was occupied while a longer-term policy was worked out. Before the government's downfall in 1880 the only decision that had been taken was that to create a British sphere of influence in southern Afghanistan by installing a chieftain at Kandahar.

When in February 1879 news reached London of a defeat for British forces in southern Africa at Isandlwana at the hands of the Zulu, Beaconsfield's main concern was that it will 'reduce our Continental influence, and embarrass our finances' (Monypenny and Buckle, 6.424). He had all but ignored southern African affairs since 1874, and had left them in the hands of successive colonial secretaries; they, in turn, were forced by the poor state of communications to cede much initiative to local British officials. Sir Bartle Frere, the new high commissioner, unwisely provoked a clash with the Zulu as part of his plan to consolidate British power in the region. Once this had happened, Beaconsfield's concern was with British prestige. The cabinet had already agreed to send out reinforcements in order to prevent domestic criticism. Beaconsfield, fearing the loss of face, prevented the recall of Frere, for which a majority of the cabinet wished. But he also showed his displeasure with Frere and the commander of the British forces, Lord Chelmsford, by sending out Sir Garnet Wolseley to exercise supreme power in the troubled area—to the great annoyance of the queen. Beaconsfield later told her that without the fiasco in southern Africa Britain would have had the international respect necessary to settle her problems in the eastern Mediterranean more easily. In particular, he saw a connection between the African embarrassment and the protest made by the khedive of Egypt in March 1879 against British and French interference in his financial policy. Britain and France were forced to secure the khedive's abdication and to assume a dual control over Egyptian finance. As this shows, Beaconsfield and Salisbury were determined to assert Britain's influence abroad, which Beaconsfield proclaimed in November 1879 was a guarantee of continental peace. Shortly beforehand the government had reached an understanding with Austria and Germany to prevent British (and, it was also intended, French or Italian) assistance to Russia in the event of her attacking the central powers. The British thus hoped to prevent reconciliation between the three Eastern powers—which would diminish British influence at Constantinople— while maintaining good relations with France. It was in defence of an active European policy of this sort, and the search for a scientific frontier in India, that Beaconsfield sought to impress a spirit of patriotism on the British people in his Guildhall speech of November 1879, in which he proclaimed as his ministry's creed 'Imperium et Libertas' (ibid., 6.495).

Death, legacy, and assessment

6

The 1880 election: beaten by the elements

If continental influence was restored, financial health was not, and this became the government's major problem up to and at the election called in the spring of 1880. Beaconsfield later complained that it had been his misfortune to govern the country during six consecutive bad harvests, while farmers were not even compensated by high prices, because of cheap food imports. Already in the summer of 1879 he feared that agricultural bankruptcy would 'finish' the government (Monypenny and Buckle, 6.477), while by early 1880 there was considerable landlord–farmer tension, which was damaging Conservative prospects and morale. Industry was also depressed in the late 1870s, which increased urban unemployment and forced the government to look for extra revenue. The state of the economy is generally held to have been the prime cause of the Conservative defeat in 1880, a belief shared by Beaconsfield himself: 'like Napoleon, I have been beaten by the elements' (Gower, 349). Gladstone alleged that the government's costly foreign adventures and its lack of fiscal rectitude were worsening the economic climate. Income tax, 2*d*. in 1874, had been increased to 5*d*. in 1878, and in a desperate attempt to avoid defeat Beaconsfield refused to consider new taxes thereafter. Much of the money for the south African expedition was borrowed, while swingeing economies in defence were undertaken.

Beaconsfield had little choice but to base the Conservative campaign on his record as defender of national interests. However, there was no clearly visible Liberal threat to those interests, and so he chose to make his point by focusing on the Irish issue. Ireland had been a marginal question for most of the parliament, though Beaconsfield claimed to have settled the Irish university question, which had upset two governments. However, Irish MPs were now obstructing business, with some prospect of encouragement from Liberal

MPs. Beaconsfield launched the campaign with a letter to the lord lieutenant of Ireland, the duke of Marlborough, in which he claimed that influential Irishmen were attempting to sever the constitutional tie with Britain and that some Liberals might exploit this to 'challenge the expediency of the imperial character of the realm'. This prospect warranted a reminder that 'the power of England and the peace of Europe will largely depend on the verdict of the country' (Monypenny and Buckle, 6.515). His strategy was ineffective: the official leaders of the opposition were moderates whose presence reassured potential defectors; the Liberal Party remained united and the Conservatives lost the election conclusively, collecting only 238 seats. Beaconsfield resigned office on 21 April 1880 and had a farewell audience with the queen six days later, though he visited Windsor three more times that year and continued a confidential correspondence with her, which was more personal than political but by no means exclusively so.

Beaconsfield's last year

Beaconsfield was inevitably cast down by another rejection and by the new political climate. He was gloomy about the future of the landed interest and, consequently, the grand social world that had been sustained by its wealth: in 1879 he predicted the end of London seasons and of racing, that antidote to socialism (Monypenny and Buckle, 6.500). He disliked the tension between landlords and farmers and interpreted the new government's budget and Ground Game Bill as an attempt to widen it. As Conservative leader in the Lords, he worked with whig dissidents to defeat the government's Compensation for Disturbance Bill, which he saw as 'not merely an Irish measure but as the opening of a great attack on the land' (ibid., 6.582). He foresaw a 'falling empire' (ibid., 6.596), and the absence of any will in foreign policy to keep 'the democrats of Europe in check' (Gower, 350).

As after the rejection of 1868, he returned to fiction. *Endymion*, published in November 1880, had largely been written in the early 1870s; Longmans paid £10,000 for the rights, said to be the largest sum then paid for a fictional work. (This was the final step in Beaconsfield's financial rehabilitation; at his death he left a personal estate of just over £84,000, so that Andrew Montagu's mortgage could be paid off without

embarrassing the estate.) It was a survey of
British politics between 1827 and 1855, lov-
ingly recreated and emphasizing the importance
of aristocratic—especially female—social influence on political fortunes. That influence helps
a colourless, conventional, well-mannered man to
rise to the premiership; he is also assisted by not
offending the insular prejudices of a commercial
country. Beaconsfield then began what may have
become a more direct commentary on his election defeat, a sequel to *Lothair* that was unfin-
ished at his death. It is known to posterity as *Falconet*, after its anti-hero, the devout, humourless,
self-serving, self-righteous, ill-tempered politician
of that name, who is manifestly a young Gladstone. One theme is Falconet's ability to exploit
the religious sentiment of the constituencies to
assist his political ascent. The other is the emergence of a powerful nihilist movement in Europe,
fomented by secret organization, devoted to the
overthrow of civilization, but aware that it can
only achieve its ends by enlisting 'some religious faith in [its] resources' (Monypenny and
Buckle, 5.556). It is irresistible to speculate that
these two themes were to be brought together
by Falconet's becoming, for career reasons, an
unconscious promoter of the revolutionary cause

who vainly justifies his actions on religious grounds.

For most of 1880 after losing office, Beaconsfield was at Hughenden, writing either novels or a flood of letters, especially to the sisters Selina, countess of Bradford, and Anne, countess of Chesterfield. He had enjoyed an ardent friendship and remarkably revealing correspondence with both since 1873, and had often seemed to be completely dependent on their affection. He once proposed to marry the widowed Lady Chesterfield in order, as they well knew, to be nearer her younger sister, with whom he was clearly infatuated, but who was married to the master of the horse in his own government. Beaconsfield had not had a permanent house in London since giving up the residence in Whitehall Gardens (rented since 1874) in order to move into Downing Street during the Eastern crisis. In November 1880 he took a nine-year lease on 19 Curzon Street. Though he claimed to be searching for a leader to replace him in the Lords, he showed no sign of giving way to the obvious successor, Salisbury. In March 1881, having taken a drug to fortify him, he made his last significant speech in the Lords, in which he argued for the retention of

Kandahar and reverted to the fundamental theme of his later years, that the prospects for India, as for Britain's world standing generally, would be determined by 'the spirit and vigour of your Parliament' (*Selected Speeches*, 2.270).

Later that month he caught a chill which, playing on his existing chest weakness, developed into severe bronchitis. He took to his bed in Curzon Street, became progressively weaker, and died there on 19 April 1881, having declined a visit from the queen; he is said to have remarked: 'No it is better not. She would only ask me to take a message to Albert' (Blake, 747). In his will he refused a public funeral and was buried at Hughenden on 26 April, with his wife and Mrs Brydges Willyams. Three royal princes, Derby, Hartington, and other leading Liberals (but not Gladstone) attended his funeral. The queen sent two wreaths, one of fresh primroses, which she claimed were his favourite flowers (she had sent him spring blooms regularly since 1868). She visited the grave four days later and subsequently had a monument erected to him above his seat in Hughenden church, a rare compliment from a British sovereign to a subject. The inscription was bowdlerized from Proverbs: 'Kings love him that speaketh right'.

In a letter to *The Times* just before the anniversary of Disraeli's death, the Anglo-Indian Sir George Birdwood suggested that those who admired his achievements and ideals should celebrate it by wearing a primrose. The gesture was repeated in 1883, by which time it had become popular—especially among those who disapproved of the external and Irish policies of the Gladstone government. Accordingly, Drummond Wolff, an independently minded Conservative MP, suggested capitalizing on Disraeli's popularity by setting up a Primrose League, a cross-class institution celebrating monarchy, social hierarchy, chivalric values, and the volunteer spirit. This became a bulwark of local Conservative electoral organization and marked the beginning of Disraeli's extraordinary posthumous life as a Conservative icon. As both parties developed a professional organization, they needed attractive figureheads, which the burgeoning mass media assisted in projecting. A new Disraeli and Gladstone were invented, competing for commemoration on ashtrays and dishcloths. Disraeli has remained a Conservative Party hero ever since. His career had been colourful, while his sonorous, inclusive, but unspecific rhetoric was ambiguous

enough to make him a useful symbol of a remarkable variety of policies. Accordingly, his name has
often been invoked in support of ends that would
have alarmed him, such as state welfare.

The league's aim to attract middle- and lower-
class members was part of a broader strategy of
'tory democracy' within the party, to reach out to
the expanded electorate of the 1880s. Disraeli's
achievement in 1867 could help in this, and an
article in *The Times* on 18 April 1883 suggested
that he had been the first to discern 'the Conservative working man, as the sculptor perceives
the angel prisoned in a block of marble'. Even
more stress was placed on Disraeli's record as a
social reformer, as the party realized the rhetorical
attractiveness of a practical interventionist image.
The interpretation of him as a man of the people,
who had the insight to appreciate the merits
of a policy of imperial consolidation and social
reform, became widely held by Conservatives in
the 1890s. It was underpinned by the conclusion
to the six-volume biography of him begun by
W. F. Monypenny and finished after Monypenny's
death by G. E. Buckle in 1920. (However, buried
in the rest of the work is a great deal of material
about other aspects of Disraeli's ideas. It remains

the only biography to treat those ideas with anything like the importance they deserve, in a conscious effort to answer Liberal and other criticisms of his lack of convictions.)

This tory democrat myth did not survive detailed scrutiny by professional historical writing of the 1960s. Specific works by Paul Smith (1967) and Maurice Cowling (1967) demonstrated that Disraeli had little interest in a programme of social legislation and was very flexible in handling parliamentary reform in 1867. Meanwhile, Robert Blake's biography of 1966, written with enviable elegance and shrewdness, replaced the old interpretations with an insistent pragmatism. Blake paid little attention to Disraeli's ideas, and belittled his philosophy as 'romantic but basically unrealistic'. He described his views on foreign policy as 'out of touch with the realities of the day', his imperial notions of 1872 as 'casual'—though he had been articulating them for four decades—and the arguments of Young England as 'gothic rubbish' (Blake, 758, 570–71, 523, 172). Instead, he pointed up Disraeli's inconsistency, oddly suggesting that his willingness to take office under Peel in 1841 cast doubt on his sincerity in later attacking him, and that his later practice was 'essentially Peelite' (ibid., 759). This argument articulated an anachronistic but then fashionable view of nineteenth-century politics that saw Peel rather than Disraeli as the founder of the Conservative Party by basing its electoral fortunes on a 'constructive' appeal to the middle classes.

More recent work on the changing electoral and ideological contexts of Victorian politics has underlined the pre-modernity of Disraeli's political world, while undermining facile comparisons of him with Peel. There has been comparatively little interest in Disraeli's political practice, but a great deal in his fiction, his ideas, his psychological orientation, and his Jewishness. These studies have revealed problems in Blake's interpretation, and drawn attention to Disraeli's uniqueness. Some scholars have begun the attempt to integrate his ideas with his practice, but in general scepticism still abounds about the latter. There has also been considerable speculation about Disraeli's private life, which was sanitized by Monypenny and Buckle (in whose biography there is not even any coherent reference to Henrietta Sykes). One biography of 1993 suggested that Disraeli had not just extramarital affairs (which seems likely) but also two illegitimate children in the mid-1860s: a boy, Ralph, with Lady Dorothy Nevill, and a girl, Catherine Donovan (Weintraub, 427–36). It is unlikely that such allegations will ever be proved, not least because Philip Rose and later his son, as executors, deliberately destroyed many of Disraeli's letters.

Interpreting Disraeli

Throughout the twentieth century, then, interpretations of Disraeli revolved around two issues: the extent of his sympathy for democracy, and his assumed lack of principle. The decline of the 'tory democrat' interpretation, combined with the vitality of the notion that Disraeli sat loose to convictions, has had the effect of diminishing respect for his political achievement. Yet the suggestion that he was an unscrupulous charlatan was originally just as politically motivated as the heroic tory democrat interpretation (though assisted by his youthful self-exposure). It was first associated with his Peelite opponents and later with Liberals and with Disraeli's high tory enemies, who used his conduct over protection and parliamentary reform as their major examples. It also has to be said that Victorian snobbery and antisemitism,

and Liberal moralism then and since, have played
a large part in entrenching it.

It is arguable not only that both these dominant interpretations are misconceived in themselves but that they have positively hindered the attempt to understand Disraeli by leading enquirers down side-tracks. There is surely no need to cast the career of such an egotist, élitist, and parliamentary intriguer in a populist light in order to understand it. Disraeli had fixed notions about the attractiveness of a few electoral cries, such as anti-Catholicism. But he had little detailed electoral knowledge, at any rate outside the home counties and Lancashire, and though on occasion he positioned himself in accordance with these fixed notions, on many others he did not do so. In any case, all his instincts were attuned to an era before that in which elections were won by national policy initiatives. He always talked of the tories as the national and popular party, but this was in contrast to whig exclusiveness and factionalism. He believed that leadership required imaginative insight into the popular psychology, and that historically inspired patriotic and monarchical language had the potential to appeal to the British public. But his rhetoric in these areas arguably aimed not so much to exploit existing prejudices for electoral gain as to tease out a rarely articulated patriotism from beneath a dominant complacency about continental affairs; this, he believed, was the job of leadership. As for his supposed inconsistency, to say that he had to abandon his original position on protection and parliamentary reform is to say little more than that he lived in the nineteenth century. Altered perspectives were imposed on all politicians of his generation; Gladstone made a virtue of them. Disraeli retained a studied flexibility on some difficult issues (such as Catholic endowment). He also habitually romanticized and exaggerated potentially humdrum affairs. However, that was because he viewed politics not as a legislative draftsman but as an artist and sociologist. He was exceptionally anxious to develop and adhere to an individual interpretation of social and political movements. He was a first-rate politician because he upheld that individual interpretation while demonstrating a necessary expediency in parliamentary manoeuvre.

Disraeli's was not a trained university mind, and it is not surprising that more fastidious intellects have criticized his 'fatal facility in suggesting hazy theories' and his lack of 'the kind of practical

sagacity which most easily inspires Englishmen
with confidence' (*Historical Essays*, 492, 486). But
his haziness can be exaggerated. He had coherent
ideas on the importance of the land, the church,
and historic tory ideals in maintaining civilization and social cohesion, and about the threat
posed to nineteenth-century society by the (in
fact very gradual) decay of these 'traditionary
influences'. This pessimistic analysis, natural in
a romantic historian, was mitigated by a fascination with the interplay of social forces and with
the human comedy of which he was an acutely
ironic observer. His love of life and nature, his constant sense of wonder at new experiences, and his
sanguine temperament ensured that—when not
affected by a self-obsessive melancholy—he was
in a good humour with the world. In any case, he
had very limited power to arrest the development
of Victorian political society: he could do nothing
about the triumph of free trade, the decline of
the old colonial relationships, and the waning of
paternalism. For much of his life he had to accept
the broad policy assumptions laid down by Liberal
politicians.

Notwithstanding all this, Disraeli's objective was
clearly conservative: to frustrate radical initiatives

which he saw as challenging national institutions and traditions. He disparaged the raising of contentious issues (and therefore premature declarations of opinion on them) unless there was a chance of solving them. All his major political moves were designed to settle questions, to take them out of the political sphere, to prevent destructive social or parliamentary agitation. When confronted with specific problems, he sought to reduce tension between town and country, landlords and farmers, capital and labour, and warring religious sects in Britain and Ireland—in other words, to create a unifying synthesis. 'Practical' social legislation was useful to the extent that it reduced the threat of government on abstract 'socialist' and centralizing principles. Had he not made possible the 1867 Reform Act, something similar would have been enacted, but it might well not have been as conservative in its social instincts and would certainly not have been as beneficial to the Conservative Party.

It must also be remembered that one objective of the struggle of 1867 was to put the party on a better footing so that it might escape having to endure another minority government, in which there was always the danger of being forced to accept radical proposals. Before 1868 Disraeli believed that he had no choice but to work with radicals; he also believed, rightly, that he was skilful enough to do so on honourably Conservative terms. This is not to deny that he was addicted to conspiracy. Moreover, he was not an infallibly expert parliamentary operator: despite the mask of aloof imperturbability that he wore in the Commons, he was impulsive and sometimes short-sighted tactically, and his colleague Northcote remarked that he always spoiled his hand by 'overdoing something or other' (Monypenny and Buckle, 4.297). None the less, his long-term aim for the party was a position of independence. He believed that the only way in which strong government and Conservative ideas could be upheld, while constitutional and local liberties were secured, was by the maintenance of a two-party system in which parties were faithful to their ideals. The Conservative Party might easily have been swallowed in coalitions headed by whig grandees. Instead he sought Conservative leadership of a strong party that defended Burkean traditional influences against abstractions, novelties, and democratic enthusiasms. However, his theory that there should be a natural aristocratic and a natural democratic party was only partly realized in his lifetime, since propertied Liberals succeeded in keeping radicals on a tight rein.

Disraeli's political style

Disraeli certainly did not offer electors a programme of legislation, or even speak in public to any significant extent. In 1879–80 he was contemptuous of Gladstone's 'spouting all over the country, like an irresponsible demagogue', which was 'wholly inexcusable in a man who was a statesman' (Monypenny and Buckle, 6.524). After the 1880 election he asserted the right of politicians to challenge the spirit of the age, which was 'generally public sentiment' and 'frequently ... public passion' (*Hansard 3*, 255, 107–8). From the time of the Bulgarian agitation Disraeli believed that Gladstone had abandoned the politics of gentlemanliness: 'posterity will do justice to that unprincipled maniac Gladstone ... with one commanding characteristic— ... whether preaching, praying, speechifying, or scribbling—never a gentleman!' (Monypenny and Buckle, 6.67). Disraeli's beliefs and political position required him to maintain that parliament was at the centre of public life and that the guiding principle of parliament was that it was a free assembly of gentlemen. He attached immense significance to its traditions and dignity, which he upheld with studious ceremony. He attached equal importance to his image in parliament: he dyed his hair, which he carefully arranged (with increasing difficulty) to preserve the trademark curl on his forehead; he resorted only to an inadequate eye-glass to remedy chronic shortsightedness; his figure was assisted by stays, of which a glimpse could occasionally be seen protruding from his frock coat (fortunately, he had a small appetite). The basis of his power was his parliamentary influence. His performance in the Commons was never without its critics; some detected a tendency to 'false melodramatic taste' (*Historical Essays*, 486). His success there was due to his devastating capacity to discern his opponents' weak (and strong) points: his epigrammatic sarcasm increasingly intimidated them from attacking him, and dissuaded rivals from seeking to supplant him and banish him to a dangerous exile below the gangway. Disraeli held tenaciously to the party leadership in the Commons for twenty-eight years; but he did so by dint of rhetorical bravado and dextrous party management, not by exploiting his position outside parliament even to the extent that Palmerston did, let alone Gladstone. As late as 1876 Bagehot claimed that 'ten miles from London...there is scarcely any real conception of him' (ibid., 504).

Disraeli had little time for demagogic politics because of his intensely individualistic conception of political leadership. Whatever the crisis, his letters were full of boasts that he was the man who had arranged affairs, that no one else was on hand to share the responsibility, or that no one else was competent (though in public he was nearly always very supportive of his disciples, earning their loyalty). His astonishing egotism sustained him through all the rejections of his career. It was all the more effective for being tempered by adversity, preventing the bumptious flamboyance of his youth from hardening into an inflexible arrogance. He had a remarkable capacity to learn from his mistakes. His tenacity and will-power allowed him to conquer his youthful lethargy and periodic depressions; they gave him courage when isolated and defiance in defeat. The conviction of his superiority to the fools and drones whom he observed occupying high positions in society and politics never left him. He disliked the company of intellectual equals: he preferred to be surrounded by idealistic young men and, especially,

by sympathetic women who could caress his ego. *133*
He was never vindictive except when he thought
his honour had been impugned; that he regarded
as a heinous offence.

As he despised the parochialism of little men,
commercial opinions, and ecclesiastical factionalism, only his ardour for the political game
saved Disraeli from being bored by most of what
counted for politics in Britain. He sought a stage
fit for a great man: he loved to philosophize about
the fate of races, nations, and empires. Sometimes he fantasized; sometimes he stuck to out-
dated ideas; usually there was a kernel of real
insight. He reflected at length on the conflicts
and consequential radical dangers facing Europe
in a way that distanced him from insular contemporaries. He believed it essential to alter blink-
ered and comfortable domestic views of the continent; he hoped that a more patriotic public
voice would increase Britain's European clout
while keeping defence expenditure low. He was
helped by the alarms generated by the expansion
of Germany and Russia and their emergence as
rival 'empires', which encouraged acceptance of
the word in British debate. When Disraeli talked
of empire, he meant the historic and symbolic

greatness of England, exemplified by its power in Europe and its global prestige. This certainly did not necessitate territorial acquisition, especially if that illuminated military weakness. It did require an active European policy and an attitude of resistance to Russia. Disraeli was innately attracted by the merits of an assertive international stance, but, true to character, he also saw the specifics of the Eastern crisis in terms of short-term parliamentary necessity on the one hand, and the long-term aim of sustaining the aristocratic European order against militarism or revolution on the other.

The enigma

Disraeli's grandiose ideas, cynicism about human motives, and his ability to marry high rhetoric with low intrigue, make him a difficult figure to read. Many of his enthusiasms and objectives would have been more familiar to continental politicians, or to those of an earlier period, than to his British contemporaries. The radical politician John Bright took exception to his candid declaration that the search for fame brought him to parliament, though this was an eighteenth-century commonplace. His egocentricity can be seen as that of an eternally maladjusted social-climbing adolescent, or that of an unprivileged outsider forced to endure watching the social and political prizes go to lesser men with better connections. His foreign policy can be seen as a gigantic castle in the air (as it was by Gladstone), or as an overdue attempt to force the British commercial classes to awaken to the realities of European politics.

With Gladstone, Disraeli was one of the two most fascinating and complex politicians of the nineteenth century. He was hardly understood at the time, and it would be presumptuous to claim that he is fully understandable now. Neither Gladstone nor Disraeli communicated very clearly what he really felt; certainly neither understood the other. But they shared a rebelliousness against the complacency and materialism of mid-Victorian Britain. Disraeli used un-English insights to urge on England a world role befitting her power and traditional values. Given the weight of commercial, sectional, and isolationist opinion in the country, this was a task that was bound to involve more failure than victory. After his last election defeat he told the Social Democratic Federation leader H. M. Hyndman that England was 'a very difficult country to move ... and one in which there is more disappointment to be looked for than success' (Blake, 764). Disraeli certainly suffered many disappointments and rejections in his courting of the British political classes. He wanted to play both the roles that he idealized in his novels, the artist–prophet and the man of action; political circumstances conspired to ensure that he had few chances to put his insights into practice.

Even so, the conclusion must be that, though only intermittently, Disraeli still succeeded, infinitely more than anyone could have imagined, in realizing the object of political life that he set out in the poem he wrote for his wife's birthday in 1846: 'to sway the race that sways the world' (*Letters*, 4.250).

Sources

W. F. Monypenny and G. E. Buckle, *The life of Benjamin Disraeli*, 6 vols. (1910–20) · R. Blake, *Disraeli* (1966) · *Disraeli's reminiscences*, ed. H. M. Swartz and M. Swartz (1975) · *Benjamin Disraeli letters*, ed. J. A. W. Gunn and others (1982–) · *Letters of Disraeli to Lady Chesterfield and Lady Bradford*, ed. marquis of Zetland, 2 vols. (1929) · *Selected speeches of the late earl of Beaconsfield*, ed. T. E. Kebbel, 2 vols. (1882) · B. Disraeli, *Vindication of the English constitution in a letter to a noble and learned lord* (1835) · B. Disraeli, *Lord George Bentinck: a political biography* (1852) · *Disraeli, Derby and the Conservative Party: journals and memoirs of Edward Henry, Lord Stanley, 1849–1869*, ed. J. R. Vincent (1978) · *A selection from the diaries of Edward Henry Stanley, 15th earl of Derby (1826–93), between March 1869 and September 1878*, ed. J. R. Vincent, Camden Society, 5th ser., 4 (1994) · S. Bradford, *Disraeli* (1982) · J. R. Vincent, *Disraeli* (1990) · S. Weintraub, *Disraeli: a biography* (1993) · J. Ridley, *The young Disraeli* (1995) · P. Smith, *Disraeli: a brief life* (1996) · D. R. Schwarz, *Disraeli's fiction* (1979) · B. Disraeli, *Inaugural address delivered to the University of Glasgow* (1873) · *Hansard's Parliamentary debates*, 3rd ser. (1830–91) · C. Howard and P. Gordon, eds., 'The cabinet journal of Dudley Ryder, Viscount Sandon', *Bulletin of the Institute of Historical Research*, special suppl., 10 (1974) [whole issue] · *The historical essays*, ed. N. St John-Stevas (1968), vol. 5 of *The collected works of Walter Bagehot* · H. Lucy, *A diary of two parliaments: the Disraeli parliament,*

1874–1880 (1885) · J. Bryce, *Studies in contemporary biography* (1903) · R. S. Gower, *Records and reminiscences* (1903) · T. E. Kebbel, *Lord Beaconsfield and other tory memories* (1907) · *The diary of Gathorne Hardy, later Lord Cranbrook, 1866–1892: political selections*, ed. N. E. Johnson (1981) · A. Lang, *Life, letters and diaries of Sir Stafford Northcote*, 2 vols. (1890) · G. Cecil, *Life of Robert, marquis of Salisbury*, 4 vols. (1921–32) · D. J. Mitchell, *Cross and tory democracy: a political biography of Richard Assheton Cross* (1991) · J. Ogden, *Isaac D'Israeli* (1969) · M. Cowling, *1867: Disraeli, Gladstone and revolution* (1967) · P. Smith, *Disraelian Conservatism and social reform* (1967) · E. J. Feuchtwanger, *Disraeli, democracy and the tory party: conservative leadership and organization after the second Reform Bill* (1968) · R. Millman, *Britain and the Eastern question, 1875–1878* (1979) · M. Swartz, *The politics of British foreign policy in the era of Disraeli and Gladstone* (1985) · R. Stewart, *The foundation of the conservative party, 1830–1867* (1978) · R. Shannon, *The age of Disraeli, 1868–1881: the rise of tory democracy* (1992) · H. C. G. Matthew, 'Disraeli, Gladstone, and the politics of mid-Victorian budgets', *Historical Journal*, 22 (1979), 615–43 · P. R. Ghosh, 'Disraelian conservatism: a financial approach', *English Historical Review*, 99 (1984), 268–96 · P. R. Ghosh, 'Style and substance in Disraelian social reform, c.1860–80', *Politics and social change in modern Britain*, ed. P. J. Waller (1987) · M. Cowling, 'Lytton, the cabinet and the Russians, August to November 1878', *English Historical Review*, 76 (1961), 59–79 · A. Warren, 'Disraeli, the conservatives and the government of Ireland', *Parliamentary History*, 18 (1999), 45–64, 145–67 · A. Warren, 'Disraeli, the conservatives and the national church', *Parliamentary History*, 19 (2000), 96–117 · J. P. Parry, 'Disraeli and England', *Historical Journal*, 43 (2000), 699–728 · G. E. C. [G. E. Cokayne], *The complete peerage of England, Scotland, Ireland, Great Britain, and the United Kingdom*, 8 vols. (1887–98); new edn, ed. V. Gibbs and others, 14 vols. in 15 (1910–98)

Index

Enjoy biography? Explore more than 55,000 life stories in the Oxford Dictionary of National Biography

The biographies in the 'Very Interesting People' series derive from the *Oxford Dictionary of National Biography*—available in 60 print volumes and online.

To find out about the lives of more than 55,000 people who shaped all aspects of Britain's past worldwide, visit the *Oxford DNB* website at **www.oxforddnb.com**.

There's lots to discover ...

Read about remarkable people in all walks of life—not just the great and good, but those who left a mark, be they good, bad, or bizarre.

Browse through more than 10,000 portrait illustrations— the largest selection of national portraiture ever published.

Regular features on history in the news—with links to biographies—provide fascinating insights into topical events.

Get a life ... by email

Why not sign up to receive the free *Oxford DNB* 'Life of the Day' by email? Entertaining, informative, and topical biographies delivered direct to your inbox—a great way to start the day.

Find out more at www.oxforddnb.com

'An intellectual wonderland for all scholars and enthusiasts'

Tristram Hunt, *The Times*

The finest scholarship on the greatest people...

Many leading biographers and scholars have contributed articles on the most influential figures in British history: for example, Paul Addison on Winston Churchill, Patrick Collinson on Elizabeth I, Lyndall Gordon on Virginia Woolf, Christopher Ricks on Alfred Tennyson, Frank Barlow on Thomas Becket, Fiona MacCarthy on William Morris, Roy Jenkins on Harold Wilson.

'Paul Addison's Churchill ... is a miniature masterpiece.'

Piers Brendon, *The Independent*

Every story fascinates...

The *Oxford DNB* contains stories of courage, malice, romance, dedication, ambition, and comedy, capturing the diversity and delights of human conduct. Discover the Irish bishop who was also an accomplished boomerang thrower, the historian who insisted on having 'Not Yours' inscribed on the inside of his hats, and the story of the philanthropist and friend of Dickens Angela Burdett-Coutts, who defied convention by proposing to the Duke of Wellington when he was seventy-seven and she was just thirty. He turned her down.

'Every story fascinates. The new ODNB will enrich your life, and the national life.'

Matthew Parris, *The Spectator*

www.oxforddnb.com

At 60,000 pages in 60 volumes, the *Oxford Dictionary of National Biography* is one of the largest single works ever printed in English.

The award-winning online edition of the *Oxford DNB* makes it easy to explore the dictionary with great speed and ease. It also provides regular updates of new lives and topical features.

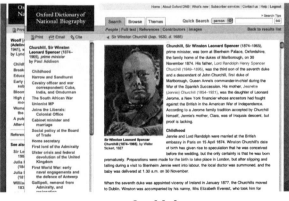

www.oxforddnb.com

The *Oxford Dictionary of National Biography* was created in partnership with the British Academy by scholars of international standing.

It was edited by the late Professor H. C. G. Matthew, Professor of Modern History, University of Oxford, and Professor Sir Brian Harrison, Professor of Modern History, University of Oxford, with the assistance of 14 consultant editors and 470 associate editors worldwide.

Dr Lawrence Goldman, Fellow and Tutor in Modern History, St Peter's College, Oxford, became editor in October 2004.

What readers say

'The *Oxford DNB* is a major work of reference, but it also contains some of the best gossip in the world.'

John Gross, *Sunday Telegraph*

'A fine genealogical research tool that allows you to explore family history, heredity, and even ethnic identity.'

Margaret Drabble, *Prospect*

'The huge website is superbly designed and easy to navigate. Who could ask for anything more?'

Humphrey Carpenter, *Sunday Times*

www.oxforddnb.com